Allen Scott

Chronicles of the great rebellion

From the beginning of the same until the fall of Vicksburg

Allen Scott

Chronicles of the great rebellion
From the beginning of the same until the fall of Vicksburg

ISBN/EAN: 9783337208073

Printed in Europe, USA, Canada, Australia, Japan

Cover: Foto ©ninafisch / pixelio.de

More available books at **www.hansebooks.com**

CHRONICLES

OF THE

GREAT REBELLION

FROM

THE BEGINNING OF THE SAME

UNTIL THE

FALL OF VICKSBURG.

BY

Rev. ALLEN M. SCOTT, D. D.

SEVENTH EDITION.

CINCINNATI:
C. F. VENT & CO., NO. 38 WEST FOURTH STREET.
1861

Entered, according to an Act of Congress, in the year 1863, by

C. F. VENT & CO.

In the Clerk's Office of the District Court of the United States, in and for the Southern District of Ohio.

CALEB CLARK, FINE LETTER-PRESS PRINTER,
CINCINNATI, O.

PREFACE.

Common Usage is Law, and Usage says, that he who writes a book must write a Preface.

The book which is here presented to the reader, gives an epitome or outline of the great Rebellion. To enter into detail, would make the work quite voluminous; and, it was considered, that at a time like the present, when momentous events are almost daily occurring, the great public cannot detain to listen to a minute detail of incidents.

At first, the author did not design to give the labors of his pen to the public. He was amid the stirring scenes of the Rebellion, and though a civilian and an old man, often has he, within the last two years, heard the roar of artillery, and witnessed the evolutions of soldiers going forth to battle. He commenced the "Chronicles" with no other motive than to beguile the hours of leisure, that, with the loss of business incident to the war, lay heavily upon him. A few friends saw some of the chapters, and expressed much pleasure at their perusal. He was afterwards induced to allow their publication in a Memphis daily paper, and it was soon apparent, that the style was pleasing to the masses, for it was impossible to supply the demand for the numbers of the paper containing these chapters. Influenced by the anxiety of the populace as thus manifested, the author has revised the "Chronicles," and added many chapters, and now in the form here presented gives them to the public.

"Why have they been written in Scripture style?" inquires some honest and inquisitive reader. I answer, Because the style is quaint, unusual, and from its novelty, calculated to make a lasting impression on the mind.

But, perhaps, it is suggested, that the style is that of the Holy Scriptures, and that its use at the present day, is sacrilegious. In answer, I will say, that the style was anciently not confined to the Holy Scriptures, but generally adopted in profane as well as sacred writings, and it is yet used in law forms and documents, and no one, I presume, would venture to say that the language in a deed or mortgage, although of the ancient or solemn style, is sacrilegious. The author venerates the Holy Bible, and takes it as the man of his council, and the guide of his life, and no one would be more averse to sacrilege than himself.

If it would be sacrilegious to use the form of speech that Moses, and the prophets, and the apostles used, it would be equally sacrilegious to wear sandals or turbans because they wore them.

In conclusion, the author would express the hope, that this cruel war of brothers—this war against the government of our fathers and the old flag that waved over us in the past, may soon be succeeded by a lasting peace, and that the wonted prosperity and happiness may ere long be fully restored.

ALLEN M. SCOTT.

MEMPHIS, TENN., October, 1863.

CONTENTS.

CHAPTER I.
Condition of the Country during the Reign of James, surnamed Buchanan.................... 15

CHAPTER II.
Resignation of James.. 18

CHAPTER III.
Nomination of a New Chief Ruler...................... 21

CHAPTER IV.
Nomination of a New Chief Ruler, (continued)...... 25

CHAPTER V.
About Abraham.. 25

CHAPTER VI.
The Election of Chief Ruler............................... 30

CHAPTER VII.
Secession of South Carolina............................... 33

CHAPTER VIII.
War Declared.. 37

CHAPTER IX.
The South Blockaded....................................... 42

CHAPTER X.
Battle of Manassas... 46

CHAPTER XI.
Generals Pillow and Polk.................................. 50

CONTENTS.

CHAPTER XII.
General Polk at Memphis.................................... 55

CHAPTER XIII.
Hard Times in Dixie.. 58

CHAPTER XIV.
Commissioners sent to Europe.......................... 61

CHAPTER XV.
Andrew Johnson... 66

CHAPTER XVI.
Emerson Etheridge... 69

CHAPTER XVII.
Battle of Belmont... 72

CHAPTER XVIII.
Boss Hale... 74

CHAPTER XIX.
General McClellan... 80

CHAPTER XX.
Fort Henry... 83

CHAPTER XXI.
Fort Donelson... 86

CHAPTER XXII.
Surrender of Nashville..................................... 91

CHAPTER XXIII.
Battle of Shiloh... 94

CHAPTER XXIV.
Battle of Shiloh, (continued)............................. 97

CHAPTER XXV.
Capture of New Orleans...................................100

CHAPTER XXVI.
Evacuation of Columbus...................................105

CHAPTER XXVII.
Fall of Fort Pillow and Fall of Memphis...............109

CONTENTS.

CHAPTER XXVIII.
Federal Dominion in Memphis..................113

CHAPTER XXIX.
George Drury and Ellen Grainger..................115

CHAPTER XXX.
George Drury and Ellen Grainger, (continued).....119

CHAPTER XXXI.
Cotton Burning..................124

CHAPTER XXXII.
Federal Conquest of West Tennessee..................129

CHAPTER XXXIII.
Contrabands..................133

CHAPTER XXXIV.
Efforts to take Richmond..................136

CHAPTER XXXV.
Holly Springs..................140

CHAPTER XXXVI.
General Price..................143

CHAPTER XXXVII.
The Guerrillas..................146

CHAPTER XXXVIII.
Taking the Oath..................149

CHAPTER XXXIX.
Adventures of Two Young Secesh..................152

CHAPTER XL.
The Conscription..................155

CHAPTER XLI.
Vicksburg, Miss..................158

CHAPTER XLII.
Siege of Vicksburg..................161

CHAPTER XLIII.
Bragg invades Kentucky..................164

CONTENTS.

CHAPTER XLIV.
John H. Morgan 168

CHAPTER XLV.
Escape of a Rebel Conscript................................171

CHAPTER XLVI.
Duvall goes to Dixie for his family.....................176

CHAPTER XLVII.
Hon. H. Stephens..179

CHAPTER XLVIII.
Brigadier Jeff...182

CHAPTER XLIX.
Peggy and Little Jimmy......................................185

CHAPTER L.
Clinton, whose surname was Chase....................191

CHAPTER LI.
Lake Providence..195

CHAPTER LII.
Startling Intelligence..199

CHAPTER LIII.
Sensation...203

CHAPTER LIV.
The Escape..205

CHAPTER LV.
Southern Divines..209

CHAPTER LVI.
Lee Marches into Maryland................................213

CHAPTER LVII.
Abraham's Warning..217

CHAPTER LVIII.
Battle at Corinth...220

CHAPTER LVIX.
Battle at Perryville...222

Contents.

CHAPTER LX.
Cane Hill and Perry Grove........................225

CHAPTER LXI.
Bombardment of Fredricksburg.................227

CHAPTER LXII.
Sherman's Attack on Vicksburg..................230

CHAPTER LXIII.
Stone River..232

CHAPTER LXIV.
Parson Brownlow......................................235

CHAPTER LXV.
Parson Brownlow, (continued)..................238

CHAPTER LXVI
The Old Miller of Nashville.......................242

CHAPTER LXVII.
The Edict of Emancipation 245

CHAPTER LXVIII.
Greenbacks 248

CHAPTER LXIX
Northern Prosperity..................................251

CHAPTER LXX.
Negro Troops...253

CHAPTER LXXI.
Running the Blockade...............................256

CHAPTER LXXII.
Bread Riots..260

CHAPTER LXXIII.
Vance's Appeal..263

CHAPTER LXXIV.
Fort Sumter Bombarded...........................266

CHAPTER LXXV.
Union Meetings..269

CHAPTER LXXVI.
Chancellorville 271

CHAPTER LXXVII.
Stoneman's Raid 274

CHAPTER LXXVIII.
Vallandigham 277

CHAPTER LXXIX.
More About Clement 280

CHAPTER LXXX.
Port Gibson 282

CHAPTER LXXXI.
John Bull and Louis Napoleon 284

CHAPTER LXXXII.
Grierson's Splendid Ride 288

CHAPTER LXXXIII.
Grand Charge on Vicksburg 292

CHAPTER LXXXIV.
Arbitrary Arrests 296

CHAPTER LXXXV.
Death of Jackson 299

CHAPTER LXXXVI.
Lee Invades Pennsylvania 301

CHAPTER LXXXVII.
The Call for Militia 303

CHAPTER LXXXVIII
The K. G. C. 306

CHAPTER LXXXIX.
Good Works 309

CHAPTER XC.
Speculation 312

CHAPTER XCI.
Privateering 315

CHAPTER XCII.
The Foreign Element...318

CHAPTER XCIII.
The $300 Clause..321

CHAPTER XCIV.
Black Troops...324

CHAPTER XCV.
East and West..327

CHAPTER XCVI.
Battle of Gettysburg.—First Day....................................331

CHAPTER XCVII.
Battle of Gettysburg.—Second Day...................................334

CHAPTER XCVIII.
Battle of Gettysburg.—Third Day....................................336

CHAPTER XCIX.
Bragg Retreats from Chattanooga....................................339

CHAPTER C.
Vicksburg Falls..341

CHAPTER CI.
Thanksgiving Psalms..344

CHRONICLES OF THE GREAT REBELLION.

CHAPTER I.

1. Now it came to pass in those days, when James, whose surname is Buchanan, was chief ruler of the land, the people were grieved because their wise men, whom they had chosen, feared not God, but were wicked in His sight.

2. Many of them had gathered themselves together at the great Sanhedrim, at the city of Washington, for the people had said unto them, "Go up hither and make laws for us and manage our affairs for us, that it may be well for us and our little ones."

3. And they went up to the great city, and communed with James, and took their seats in the great Sanhedrim, even in the Congress of the United States.

4. And behold these were the days of peace and prosperity. The lands of the people were fruitful, and their barns were full of corn. They were arrayed in

...ine linen and much crinoline, and fared sumptuously every day.

5. And the people had built them many railroads, and put upon them great chariots that belched forth fire and smoke; and the chariots were of great size, and made of iron and wood curiously carved, and brass and steel.

6. Moreover, these chariots did fly upon the roads of iron, swift as an eagle, and men did travel upon them, and carried many parcels of oil, and wine, and spice, and fine flour.

7. And they carried much cotton, and tobacco, and lambs' wool, and curious vessels of wood, and iron, and brass.

8. And their cities did grow and become mighty upon the earth, and their fame went abroad into all the earth.

9. Then did the magicians stretch out long wires of iron, reaching from one city to another, which they called Telegraphs, and by means of magnetism they did send tidings one to another, even as men speak face to face.

10. And the people became proud, and they said

one to another, "There is no people upon the face of the whole earth that is equal unto us, not even the land of Britain, whence our fathers came."

11. And their young men became haughty, and learned to chew tobacco, and to smoke cigars, and to drink wine, and costly drinks. Moreover they were profane before men, and foolish, and cared not to be as wise as their fathers were.

12. And the maidens likewise were exceedingly puffed up, and they wore costly merchandise, and rings and bracelets of gold, and jewels and precious stones, and they arrayed themselves in silk and fine apparel, insomuch that none had ever witnessed the like in any part of the earth.

13. And the wise men at Washington drank wine, and became drunken, and they spent the people's money in riotous living, and failed to make wise laws by which the land should be governed.

14. Then were there such examples of corruption as had not been seen upon the earth since the days of Noah; for men stole vast sums from the treasury, and gave bribes unto judges and juries, and they slew one another, and their crimes filled the land with mourning.

CHAPTER II.

1. Now James, the Chief Ruler, was an old man and full of years.

2. And when he perceived that his eyes were dim and his strength well nigh gone, he called together the wise men, and said unto them,—

3. Men and Brethren, ye perceive that I am an old man, for my locks are white as hoar frost, and my knees tremble because of many years.

4. Ye know that I have served the country from my youth, and, now, behold I need rest in my old age!

5. Look ye among yourselves, and choose one to be the Chief Ruler of this mighty nation after me, for I must soon be gathered unto my fathers.

6. Moreover, James told them that on the fourth day of the month, at the end of the fourth year of his reign, even on that self-same day, would he leave the City of Washington, and cease to be the Chief Ruler of the land forever.

7. Then were the wise men so vexed, and they lifted up their voice and wept; for they loved James; he had been to them as a father, and when they had taken much gold and silver from the treasury, he had not punished them.

8. And they fell upon his neck and kissed him. And they departed each man to his own house.

9. Now, the wise men from the South, communed one with another, and consulted whom they should choose to be Chief Ruler.

10. And they agreed to come together at the city of Charleston, and to ask the elders of all the Southern country to meet them, that they might deliberate together, and choose one who would favor the people of the Southern States.

11. Then they sent word into all the South, for the people to choose discreet men, who should go to Charleston, and sit together in a convention.

12. The wise men from the North, heard of the doings of the wise men of the South, and they said, "Let us hold a convention among ourselves, and choose a Chief Ruler from the North, that it may be well with us and with our party.

13. And they appointed a convention at the lake city, even the city of Chicago, and sent a proclamation into all the land, inviting the elders from all the provinces of the North, to come unto that place.

CHAPTER III.

1. Now it came to pass when it was noised abroad throughout the land, that James, whose surname is Buchanan, would soon be Chief Ruler no more, there arose great contention among the people.

2. Some of them cried out, saying, let us appoint John, whose surname is Bell, for he is a mighty man, full of wisdom, and well suited to be the Chief Ruler of a great nation.

3. Others say, nay, but we will choose John, whose surname is Breckenridge, for he loved our nation, and hath done many mighty deeds for it.

4. Now, this John dwelt in the land of Kentucky, and he was a man of great repute in the land; he was comely to look upon, and eloquent in speech.

5. Moreover, he had long been the companion of James, and knew how to be Chief Ruler, for he had been second in office for many years.

6. Meantime, the people of the North, said among

themselves, whom shall we choose? for there were many among them that wished to be Chief Ruler.

7. There was one among them, who was fair spoken, and well versed in all the manners and customs of this "universal Yankee nation," and his name was William, but in the Anglo-Saxon tongue he was called Seward.

8. And William greatly desired to be chosen Chief Ruler. So he communed with Horace, the High Priest of the Tribune in the city of Gotham.

9. And Horace loved William, and his soul clave unto him. And William said unto Horace, swear unto me that thou wilt be true unto me, and that the Tribune will favor my election.

10. And Horace sware unto him. And William gave Horace much gold, and some oil in a censor, and a pomegranate, and kissed him, and departed unto his own house.

11. And Horace wrote in the Tribune advising the people to choose William for their Chief Ruler. He also made many speeches, and showed how much William loved the country—how well he had filled the place of Governor of New York, and how powerfully he had opposed Southern slavery.

12. And the thing pleased the Abolitionists, and they swore upon the palms of their hands, and cried out, great and mighty is William, whose surname is Seward!

13. Meanwhile the people of the South gathered together in all the States, and cities, and towns, and villages, and they choose good and discreet men to go to Charleston, to nominate some one to be Chief Ruler of the land.

14. In these days it came to pass, that there was a man in the tribe of Illinois, whose name was Stephen, which in the tongue of the Suckers, means, the Little Giant.

15. Stephen was a man of small stature; but he was comely to look upon. He was eloquent in speech, fond of champaigne and Democratic principles.

16. Stephen was a man of great authority. Once upon a time the people had chosen him for a Judge, and then they had sent him to Congress from the gallant Sucker State.

17. So great was the fame of Stephen, that there was none like him, in all the North-West, nor was there any so powerful in all the land.

18. About this time many editors wrote in the newspapers, saying, "Let us make Stephen Chief Ruler," and the saying greatly pleased the people.

CHAPTER IV.

1. And when the time had come for the elders to assemble at Charleston, to nominate a candidate for the Presidency,

2. Behold they came from all parts, some wishing to nominate John, whose surname is Bell; others preferring John the Kentuckian.

3. Then came friends of William, saying,

4. Choose ye William to be Chief Ruler, and I will give unto you each a fine suit of purple, and a Federal office, and your little ones shall live upon the fat of the land.

5. But the friends of Stephen came, saying, "Let your choice fall upon Stephen, and great good shall come unto us, and upon you, and upon all that dwell in North America.

6. Then great fear fell upon the Convention, for they were sore vexed. They knew not whom to choose, and the thing was a great trial unto them.

7. And they made speeches and cast lots for many days. And their wrath one toward another waxed warm, and they failed to choose one to be Chief Ruler. Then they arose and went each man to his own house.

8. Then the friends of John, whose surname is Bell, made a league that they would vote for him, and no other; and so he was their candidate.

9. And the friends of John, the Kentuckian, also made a league to vote for him, and he came forth as a candidate for Chief Ruler.

10. Then gathered the elders of the North together at the city of Chicago, to choose one to be Chief Ruler over all the land.

11. And they came from the tribe of Maine, and Massachusetts, and Minnesota, and from all the country north of Mason and Dixon's line.

12. And when they were gathered together, Horace read them a letter from William, and said unto them: "Men and brethren, I pray you, if I have found favor in your sight, nominate William this day." And he bowed himself unto the earth three times.

13. Then came there one and stood up in the midst,

and beckoned with his hand, and they gave audience unto him.

14. And he said unto them, that he came unto them from Abraham, whose surname was Lincoln, who was of the tribe of Kentucky,

15. That Abraham had sent unto them, saying, "Nominate me this day, and I will promise you that I will give great gifts unto all that will vote for me."

16. And this saying pleased the people, and they nominated Abraham to be Chief Ruler.

CHAPTER V.

1. Now Abraham was a man tall in stature, and his complexion was as dark as an Ethiopian.

2. And Abraham dwelt in the region of the Sangamon river, and drank its waters, and was brought up as a "splitter of rails."

3. And Abraham was two score and fourteen years old when he was nominated for Chief Ruler.

4. It came to pass when a mighty rumor went out through all the land, Behold the Chicago convention hath nominated Abraham,

5. That the friends of Stephen assembled together, and said one to another, Let us nominate Stephen, for he once did beat Abraham for the Senate, peradventure he may beat him again.

6. And they did accordingly, and they nominated Stephen.

7. Then many persons left their houses, and went

through all the land, and made speeches, and wrote circulars, and paid money.

8. And they gave promises and pledges, and they made threats, if the people should not give their votes to their friends.

9. And great excitement prevailed, such as no man in all the land had ever seen.

10. And some wore badges, and emblems, and medals.

11. And they dreamed dreams, and they swore oaths, and greatly disturbed the public peace.

12. And many were there of the South, that swore in their wrath, that if Abraham should be chosen to be Chief Ruler, they would withdraw from the Union.

13. In those days, there were societies known as the "Wide Awakes," and "Plug Uglies."

14. Some of the baser sort wore brass knuckles; others carried repeaters or derringers. Murders were committed, and assaults were made, and men's hearts failed them through fear.

CHAPTER VI.

1. Now it came to pass in the third year of the reign of James, surnamed Buchanan, and in the eleventh month of the self-same year,

2. That the people assembled themselves to vote.

3. Then came the hardy sons of Maine, and they of the tribe of Vermont, and of New Hampshire, and of the Bay State,

4. And of Rhode Island, and the land of patent clocks and wooden nutmegs,

5. And they did cast their votes by fifties, and by hundreds, and by thousands;

6. And the people of the great States of New York and Pennsylvania, and also New Jersey, and little Dela, flocked to the poles, and voted.

7. And the people of the South, where tobacco, and cotton, and rice, are cultivated, and where there are many of the sons and daughters of Ham, voted;

8. And the people of the North-West, even the

Buckeyes, Hoosiers, and Suckers; Wolverines and Hawkeyes, from all the region of prairies, and lakes, and even beyond the Mississippi, came to the polls and voted for Chief Ruler.

9. And the wrath of men waxed warm, and they drank cheap whisky and lager beer, and behold their patriotism boiled over.

10. And when the sun went down, there were drunken men not a few, and some had bloody noses and mashed mouths.

11. Then were tidings sent upon the wires, and all men everywhere greatly desired to hear the news.

12. No man saluted his neighbor, saying, how doest thou? or is it well with thee and thy little ones?

13. For no man cared for aught else than the result of the election.

14. Now when the morrow was come, and the votes had been counted, behold Abraham was elected.

15. Then did the people of the North rejoice. They illuminated their cities, and made orations, and sang songs, and gave gifts one unto another.

16. Then sent they unto Horace, saying, Write us, we pray thee, a Psalm, that we may sing and be merry

17. And Horace wrote them a Psalm, and the people sang it, and their voice was as the sound of many waters.

CHAPTER VII.

SECESSION OF SOUTH CAROLINA.

1. When the people of South Carolina heard that Abraham was elected, they rent their clothes and put on sackcloth and ashes.

2. And they cried one to another, saying, Alas! for us, for we are undone.

3. Then came certain together at Columbia, the capital of the Palmetto State, and they communed one with another.

4. And they said, Let others do as they may, but as for us, we will secede from the Union!

5. Then did they pull down the old flag, even tho flag of their fathers, the flag that had protected them in their infancy, and had made the country prosperous and happy.

6. And they tore the flag into fragments and trode upon it.

7. And they said, let no man henceforth celebrate the fourth of July, for behold the Union is dissolved.

8. And South Carolina seceded from the Union, and her wise men left Washington and went each man to his own house.

9. When the other States of the South, heard that South Carolina had seceded, they were sore vexed.

10. For they said, South Carolina is our Sister; Her people are bone of our bone and flesh of our flesh, and our souls do cleave unto her.

11. Abraham will send an armed host to subdue her, and burn up her cities, and lay waste her rice-fields, and carry away her negroes;

12. Let us arise and secede, and join with South Carolina, and build up a great Southern Confederacy.

13. And we will have a President, and a Congress of our own, and no more depend upon the "Yankees" of the North;

14. We will no more send them our cotton, or tobacco, or rice; nor will we ever buy goods of them again;

15. For the days of patent clocks, and nutmeg gritters, and Yankee school ma'ams, are at an end.

16. Then did Alabama, and Mississippi, and Georgia, and Florida, and Louisiana, and Texas secede from the Union;

17. And they seized upon the Forts and Arsenals of the South, and the guns, and cannon, and all the implements of war.

18. And there was great commotion among the people; for there were many that loved the Union, and were loth to give up the government of their fathers.

19. For they said where shall we find a better? Have we not prospered? Has not our domain extended until it reaches from ocean to ocean? and have we not grown to be great among the nations of the earth?

20. But the friends of Secession, answered and said Ye speak as fools and not as wise men. Know ye not that Abraham is elected, and that he will have a free-soil cabinet? His administration will do nothing for the South, but much against it, and we will not submit to it.

21. And the friends of the Union, said, We did not vote for Abraham, and lament that he was elected; but we know that he cannot do us much hurt, if we

remain in the Union. The Constitution and the laws will protect us.

22. Then were the Secessionists angry, and they said, ye are no friends to the South, if ye speak thus. They that are not for us are against us.

23. And they sent out a proclamation into all the land of the South, for all who loved the old flag, and did not wish to see it demolished to remove from the South in forty days.

24. Then were there lamentation and great sorrow; for men were compelled to leave their homes, and the ashes of kindred and loved ones,

25. And to become exiles and strangers, and wanderers in forests and desert places, and caves of the earth, and dens.

26. Now, there were Vigilant Committees in all the South, and they ceased not night and day to seek after all that loved the Union, and to cast them into prison.

27. Some they tarred and feathered; they shaved the heads of some; and they beat some, and some they hanged to a tree.

CHAPTER VIII.

WAR DECLARED.

1. These were but the beginning of sorrow, for the times grew worse and worse, until no one in all the land of Dixie, dared to speak in behalf of the land of his fathers.

2. Now, when James had served his full time, Abraham came to the Federal city, and delivered a great oration, and became the Chief Ruler of the land.

3. Then came there Commissioners from the South, and they said unto him, Let there be no strife between thee and us, for behold all we are brethren!

4. Let us, we pray thee, separate peaceably; and we will build up a great nation, and be friends, and trade together, and get great gain.

5. But Abraham said, nay, but I have sworn to support the Constitution, and cannot give up so much

of the soil of this Union, as a dove may need for her feet! I will not allow you to secede from the Union!

6. Then the Commissioners from the South, arose and departed from Abraham, and brought word to their friends.

7. And they said, we will have a war with Abraham, for he will not allow us to secede.

8. Then Abraham sent his proclamation into all the land, calling for 75,000 spearmen, and horsemen and footmen, and archers and slingers, to gather themselves together, to suppress the Great Rebellion.

9. Now, Arkansas, Tennessee, North Carolina, and Virginia had not seceded, but still clave to the Union;

10. But when they saw that Abraham was collecting an army to subdue their brethren of the South, their wrath was kindled;

11. And when he sent unto the Governor's of these States for aid against the South, they would not furnish it.

12. And these States seceded from the Union, and joined themselves unto South Carolina, and the other Southern States.

13. About this time a meeting of the mighty men

of the South was held at Montgomery, which is a city of no mean repute in Alabama.

14. And these mighty men of the South did proceed to form a provisional government, which they called the Confederate States of America, and they chose that city for the capital.

15. Now, there was one Jefferson, whose surname was Davis, of the tribe of Mississippi. He was a valiant man, for he had been in the Mexican War, and had married Gen. Taylor's daughter.

16. He was a member of the great Sanhedrim at Washington, as Senator from his own tribe, and he was opposed to Abraham, and greatly in favor of Secession.

17. Him they chose for Provisional President of the Confederate States, and he made an oration to the people and greatly encouraged them.

18. And they fell upon their faces, and for the space of three hours, ceased not to cry, "*Hurrah! Jeff. Davis and the South.*"

19. And Jefferson chose wise men to be his counsellors, and appointed Brigadier and Major-Generals for the army.

20. And the whole country was stirred up, and prepared to go to War. It was the theme by day, and the song by night.

21. Grave Senators and Reverend Divines made orations, and urged the people to rise up and discard the government of their fathers.

22. Farmers abandoned their furrowed fields, and caused their pruning hooks to be made into Bowie knives, and their lands lay idle, and brought forth nothing to support man and beast.

23. Mechanics left their shops, teachers gave up their schools, colleges closed their doors, ministers came down from their pulpits, and all prepared themselves to go forth to war;

24. And Jefferson commanded to send men through all the land to seize all the rifles, and shot-guns, and muskets, and pistols, and Bowie knives.

25. And all that were cunning workmen, wrought day and night, in mending and making guns, and knives, and swords, and drums;

26. And the women through all the region of the South, made flags having on them, "the Stars

and Bars," and they made clothes for the soldiers, and haversacks, and they gave them blankets, and bread, and much wine.

CHAPTER IX.

THE SOUTH BLOCKADED.

1. Now, it came to pass, that when Abraham heard of the doings of the South, that his wrath was kindled.

2. And he commanded all the mails to Dixie to cease, so that no one could send a letter to the South, or to the North.

3. And he sent his ships of war to blockade all the Southern ports, that no ships from England or France could go to them with bread or wine, or great guns, or powder, or percussion caps;

4. And Abraham gave commandment, that no ship from the South should go out upon the sea, to carry cotton to other lands, or to bring back merchandize.

5. Then did Jefferson and the men of the South, send abroad in all the land, to the merchants and others who were indebted to the people of the North, greeting;

6. And commanded them that they should not pay

them any silver or gold, or bank-bills, or cotton, or corn, or wine;

7. But all that were indebted to the North were commanded to make payment to the Confederate States, and all property in the South, belonging to men of the North, was confiscated.

8. Now, the tribe of Virginia was very ancient, and it reached from the sea toward the West, even to the Ohio river;

9. And this tribe was rich in tobacco, and wheat, and barley, and lambs' wool;

10. And, moreover, it had many great ships, and banks of money, and manufacturers without number;

11. And the schools and colleges of Virginia were of great renown, so that there were none like them upon the face of the whole earth.

12. And the sons of Virginia were brave, and her daughters were fair and beautiful to look upon.

13. And there were scholars, and orators, and poets, and mighty statesmen in Virginia.

14. It was in Virginia, that Washington, the father of his country was born, and his ashes repose upon her bosom.

15. It was in Virginia, that Patrick Henry, surnamed the eloquent, was born, and lived, and died.

16. It was in Virginia, that Madison, and Jefferson, and Tyler, and Wirt, and John Randolph lived; for Virginia was called the "Mother of Presidents."

17. It was in Virginia, that John Brown ended his eventful career.

18. The people of Virginia, especially such as belonged to the "first families" thereof, were haughty, and walked with out-stretched necks and made a mincing with there feet.

19. Now, it grieved the people of Virginia, that they had not elected a President from that tribe, and they murmured at the South because of this.

20. Then Jefferson called together his wise men, and sooth-sayers, and astrologers, and horse-doctors, and advised them to conciliate Virginia, by locating the Capital of the Confederacy at Richmond their chief city.

21. And the saying pleased the wise men, and they commanded that Richmond should be the capital.

22. And Jefferson, and his counsellors, and mighty

men arose and went unto Richmond, and there they abode.

23. And they, issued bills of credit, which the people called "Confederate money," and Jefferson gave commandment, to cast into prison, any man who should refuse to accept this money in the payment of debts due to him.

24. And behold the land was flooded with Confederate money, for it was more plentiful than ever the locusts were in Egypt.

CHAPTER X.

BATTLE AT MANASSAS.

1. MEANWHILE Abraham was collecting a mighty host. There were captains of fifties, and captains of hundreds, and colonels, and majors, and brigadiers without number.

2. And Abraham set over all these, Winfield, whose surname was Scott. Winfield was an old man, well stricken in years, and his locks were as lambs' wool.

3. He was like unto Saul in stature, and was known in all the earth for his skill in war, for he had been in war in Mexico, and was a famous chieftain.

4. Winfield had command of all Abraham's army, and resolved to march to Richmond, and to seize Jefferson and all his wise men.

5. When Jefferson heard what Winfield wished to do, he collected a great army near Richmond.

6. In this army, he had many thousands from the

South, and also from Virginia, and all parts of the Southern Confederacy.

7. Now, there was a certain man, named *Beauregard*, of French decent, and he dwelt in the tribe of Louisania. He was a man of great discretion and valor, and well skilled in all the arts of war.

8. Him Jefferson had made a Major-General, and placed him over the army.

9. Now there is a place in Virginia, where two railroads meet, and there are mountains on each side, so that an army cannot go round to the right or the left.

10. And this place is on the main road as one goes from Washington City to Richmond, and a great creek flows hard by, which is called in the Anglo-Saxon, *Bull Run*, but in the English tongue, it is called *Manassas Gap*.

11. Here Gen. Beauregard resolved to make a stand, and fight with Winfield.

12. And Winfield knew Gen. Beauregard, for the latter had served as a lieutenant under Winfield, in the Mexican War, and Winfield knew that he was brave and well skilled in all that pertains to war.

13. But Winfield said to himself, Behold I am a veteran, a hero even of two wars; what need I care for this Gaul, who in comparison, is a mere strippling? I will go forth against him, and vanquish him, and march into Richmond.

14. And it came to pass in the first year of the reign of Abraham, and in the seventh month, and on the twenty-first day of the self-same month, Winfield marched forth his mighty hosts against Beauregard.

15. Then came there many from Washington, both men and women, to see the great battle, and they stood afar off, and looked on.

16. And the battle commenced in the morning, and it waxed warm, and the roar of the artillery, and of small arms, and the tumult of battle, was great;

17. And many were the slain in each army, and the blood ran in rivulets, and the ground was covered with the fallen slain,

18. And when it was now past noon, reinforcements came to the Confederates, and they fought with great valor, and Winfield's forces gave way, and fled;

19. And the Confederates pursued them, and slew a great multitude of them, and captured many.

20. Then was Winfield sore vexed, for he was an old man, and had fought many battles, and had never been defeated before;

21. And great fear fell upon them of Washington, lest the Confederates should come and burn up their city, and destroy the capital of the nation;

22. And the Confederates took captive some of those who were spectators of the fight, and carried them to Richmond, and cast them into prison.

23. Then were the Confederates greatly elated, because Winfield had been defeated, and they gave great praises to Beauregard and those who were with him, in the great battle of Manassas.

CHAPTER XI.

GENS. PILLOW AND POLK.

1. Now it came to pass in those days, that Gideon, whose surname is Pillow, had been appointed a Major-General by the people of Tennessee,

2. And he came to Memphis, and had his Headquarters in that city,

3. And he gathered an army and fortified the city, and planted cannon on the river's brink.

4. Now, Memphis stands on the great Father of Waters, and is a great city, and its merchants had grown rich upon its trade and their gains;

5. Their houses were of brick, and stone, and marble, and costly materials brought from afar, and they were ornamented with wood, and gold, and silver, and precious stones.

6. And the trade in cotton and tobacco was very great, and men from all nations came to the city to

trade and get gain, and they sold silk, and fine linen, and goods of purple and scarlet.

7. The railroads came from the East, and from the West, and from the North, and from the South, and many were the steamboats, (which, being interpreted, mean floating palaces,) at the wharf at Memphis.

8. And every day was the city improving. It flourished as the green-bay tree, and bade fair to rival all the cities of the South and West.

9. But when the war came, all its prosperity was at an end. The trade with all places abroad, ceased. Commerce was prostrated, and all business, except that which pertains to war, was discontinued.

10. And the people of Memphis, surnamed the Bluff city, were in favor of Secession, and all of them save five, voted against the Union.

11. Gideon was a rank Secessionist, because he had many man-servants and maid-servants, and was a man of much wealth.

12. Moreover, he was a man of great ambition, and looked to the probabilities of his own promotion to a place of great honor, if the South could but succeed in the struggle.

13. And he hated Abraham and the North.

14. Now, there was in these days, one Leonidas, whose surname is Polk, a man of great wealth and influence among the people.

15. He was a man skilled in divers tongues, such as the Latin, Greek, and Hebrew, and he had much wisdom, and he was the Chief Priest in the tribe of Louisiana.

16. Leonidas was courteous and fair spoken, and eloquent of speech.

17. And when he was a youth, he was instructed how to use the bow, and sword, and to cast darts, and to understand all the arts of war.

18. And Jefferson knew Leonidas, and sent unto him, saying, come unto me, I pray thee, if I have found favor in thy sight.

19. And Leonidas arose, and went unto Richmond; and when he had come into the presence of Jefferson, he fell down before him, and reverenced him.

20. And Jefferson raised up Leonidas, and spake kindly unto him.

21. And he said unto him, I sent for thee, O

Leonidas, to ask thee to lay aside thy priestly garments, and to become a man of war.

22. For behold Lincoln with all his hosts of Philistines, is coming against us, to destroy our vineyards, to lay waste our fields, to burn our houses, and to carry away our negroes.

23. And Leonidas said, Live forever, O Jefferson, thou son-in-law of General Taylor. But tell me, I pray thee, how can I do this thing? for I am the Bishop of Louisiana, and my office is one of peace and not one of war and bloodshed.

24. And Jefferson lifted up his voice and said, Didst not thou receive thy instruction at West Point? And what return hast thou made to thy country for the education thus conferred upon thee?

25. I know thee, that thou art not only a wise man, but thou are valiant, and being a regular West-Pointer, thou mayst aid me in defending the South.

26. And Leonidas said, what post of honor wilt thou give me, if I agree to aid thee?

27. And Jefferson said unto Leonidas, I will make thee a Major-General, and give thee a thousand pounds

weight of gold, and thou shalt sit on my right hand, and none shall be more honorable than thou.

28. Then did Leonidas consent, and Jefferson made him a Major-General, and took a ring from his hand, and put it on Leonidas, and gave him his sword and buckler, and helmet, and spear, and blessed him, and bade him depart for the South.

29. And Leonidas got into the cars and departed for the South.

CHAPTER XII.

GEN. POLK AT MEMPHIS.

1. And it came to pass that Leonidas determined to have his Head-quarters at Memphis along with Gideon.

2. And he sent a messenger to Memphis, to tell Gideon that he was approaching, and would be in the city on the morrow

3. Then did Gideon rejoice, for he had known Leonidas many years. And he prepared a room for him at the Gayosa, and ordered them of the inn to prepare a sumptuous dinner.

4. Then went Gideon out to the Depot of the Memphis and Charleston Railroad, and waited for the coming of Leonidas.

5. And behold the cars came and brought Leonidas, and he was no more in Pontifical robes, but was arrayed as a Major-General.

6. He wore epauletts on his shoulders, and a sash round his waist, and the sword of Jefferson hung at his side.

7. And Gideon fell on his neck and embraced him. And he gave him a pomegranate, and an orange, and some wine, and the two entered a hack, and drove to the Gayosa.

8. Now, a great army from Tennessee, and Mississippi, and from Louisiana, and Alabama, had come together at Union city, a small town in Tennessee.

9. For Abraham had sent an army to Cairo in the tribe of Illinois, it being the point at which the Mississippi and Ohio rivers come together.

10. During all these days, the tribe of Kentucky had taken no part in the strife between the North and the South, but claimed to be neutral, inclining neither to the one side nor to the other.

11. And there was a city in Kentucky, on the Mississippi river, called Columbus, which the Federals and, also, the Confederates, desired to occupy, as it was a key to West Tennessee.

12. But the Governor of Kentucky sent his order into all the world, and especially into all Kentucky,

commanding all belligerents whether Federals or Confederates,

13. To keep off the sacred soil of Kentucky, or otherwise he would punish them.

14. Jefferson sent word unto Leonidas and Gideon not to invade Kentucky until the Federals did, and then to march forward and seize Columbus.

15. And not many days thereafter, Federal troops marched into Louisville, which is a city in Kentucky, and took possession thereof.

16. And when Leonidas heard thereof, he marched his forces into Columbus, and placed a garrison there.

17. And he fortified the place with a great wall and a wide ditch, and he planted many great guns upon the bank of the river.

18. And Leonidas gathered a great army at Columbus, and much corn, and bacon, and all the implements of war, and they sent out to all the people greeting, to fear nothing, that Leonidas cou'd hold Columbus against all the world.

CHAPTER XIII.

HARD TIMES IN DIXIE.

1. Inasmuch as Abraham's ships had compassed all the land, no goods could be brought into Dixie.

2. So many things which the people were accustomed to have, became exceedingly scarce, and demanded a great price.

3. For, as there are almost no manufactures in the South, and no goods could come unto them from the North, the people began to be in want.

4. Then were there many who cared not for the country, but only for themselves, whom the people call speculators, and they bought up flour and meal, and salt, and things of that kird,

5. And sold these things unto the people, at rates immensely dear, so that those who were poor could not buy;

6. And many there were that suffered greatly

because of the price of food, and of the great scarcity of corn.

7. Schools were discontinued, many churches were abandoned, and men cared not to speak of anything save the great war and its stirring events.

8. The women of the South took great interest in matters pertaining to the war. They formed societies, and made garments for the Southern soldiers, and baked cakes, and boiled hams, and sent many comforts to those who were in camp.

9. In the city of Memphis, the ladies fitted up a great house with beds, and carpets, and chairs, and invited all the soldiers that were sick, to come to that house,

10. And the ladies waited upon them, and gave them medicine, and food, and spoke kindly to them;

11. And when they recovered from sickness, they returned to the army blessing the memory of the ladies of Memphis;

12. And some there were that died, and the ladies wept at their bedside, and followed them to that narrow home prepared for all living.

13. And many of those that recovered their

strength, would have died, but for the kindness of these benevolent ladies.

14. Their great house was called "The Southern Mothers' Home," but it is now called "The Irving Prison."

15. As it was in Memphis, so was it in the North,—wives, daughters, sisters, and mothers, continued day and night to labor, to clothe and comfort those who were dear to them, and who were serving their country in the tented field.

16. And thus time rolled on, and this war progressed; a war of brothers fighting over the graves of their departed sires.

CHAPTER XIV.

COMMISSIONERS SENT TO EUROPE.

1. About this time it came to pass, that there went forth a rumor through all the land, that England and France were about to acknowledge the Independence of the South.

2. When Jefferson heard this, he called together his wise men, and advised with them, whether he should not send discreet men to London and Paris, to urge those great powers to recognition.

3. And all the wise men advised Jefferson to do that thing; and he chose two men of great discretion, and he commissioned them to go to the Court of St. James, and also to the Court of Napoleon, and do all in their power to procure favor.

4. One of these Commissioners was Mason of Virginia, and the other was Slidell of Louisiana.

5. Now, these two Commissioners had to cross the

ocean, but, all the ports in the South being blockaded, it was difficult for them to get out to sea.

6. But they ran the blockade, and arrived at Havana, a city of Cuba, surnamed "the gem of the ocean."

7. And it came to pass, that there was a British vessel at Cuba, bound for the land of Albion, and the Confederate Commissioners engaged their passage on that vessel.

8. And the vessel sailed from Cuba, and went out on the wide and deep sea, and was sailing toward the old world, with the flag of old England, streaming from her mast-head.

9. But certain messengers had gone to Abraham, and told him that Mason and Slidell had run the blockade, and were on their way across the ocean;

10. And Abraham sent word to the captains of vessels, and commanded them to watch every place on the sea, where any Confederate ship might pass, and to seize these Commissioners, and to cast them into prison;

11. Moreover, Abraham promised unto him who

should take them, a gold chain, and to sit at his table, and to drink buttermilk out of his cup.

12. Then went out all the Captains of steamships, and the Commanders of steam-tugs, and Commodores, and Admirals, and they covered the sea looking for the Confederate Commissioners;

13. And Commodore Wilkes lifted up his eyes, and beheld a ship sailing to the eastward,

14. And he pursued her, and overtook her, and demanded that the Confederate Commissioners should be surrendered to him

15. But the Captain declared that they were passengers in his ship, and under the protection of the British flag, and he was loth to give them up;

16. But Commodore Wilkes could not be appeased, and took both Mason and Slidell, and brought them to New York, and cast them into prison.

17. When the British ship reached England, and the Captain had told what Commodore Wilkes had done, John Bull was angry, and the British lion began to roar.

18. For the people of England loved their flag, and

were sore vexed because its rights had not been respected.

19. Then was Abraham alarmed lest he should have a war with England, and he communed with William, whose surname is Seward, and he told him what things had happened;

20. Now, William is a man of great cunning, and no man has ever been found, who could circumvent him;

21. And when William beheld that Abraham was troubled in spirit, and was ready to die, he was moved with compassion,

22. And he lifted up his voice, and spake kindly unto Abraham, and bade him not to fear.

23. Moreover, William said, we will send a letter to John Bull, and say that we did not authorize Commodore Wilkes to make the seizure, and then will his wrath be appeased.

24. And the saying pleased Abraham, and he released the two Commissioners, and sent a letter to the English Minister, saying, that the Government disavowed the act of Commodore Wilkes;

25. Then was John Bull reconciled, and grew merry over a bowl of punch, and smiled most graciously upon Abraham and his Cabinet.

CHAPTER XV.

ANDREW JOHNSON AND WILLIAM BROWNLOW.

1. Now as it is written in the eighth chapter of these Chronicles, Tennessee seceded along with Virginia and North Carolina.

2. Tennessee had long been known to love the South, and was regarded as acting with the Southern States in all important matters.

3. Her sons were brave and her daughters exceedingly fair and beautiful to look upon.

4. It was in Tennessee that Andrew, whose surname was "Old Hickory," dwelt, and his ashes are now resting beneath her soil.

5. It was in Tennessee that James, whose surname is Polk, had his habitation, and when he died he also was buried beneath her soil.

6. And Tennessee had become a great State. Her

border extended from the mountains in the east, hard over against North Carolina, even unto the great Mississippi river.

7. Her chief cities were built of stone, and brick and marble; her farmers had grown rich upon the fat of the land, and her merchants were like unto princes.

8. And when Tennessee seceded from the Union, there were a few among her citizens that loved Abraham and the Republicans, and refused to secede with the State.

9. Among them was Andrew, whose surname is Johnston, who dwelt in the Eastern part of the State, and he had been one of the Senators of Tennessee.

10. When he saw that Tennessee had seceded, he departed from her borders and went unto the land of Abraham, even unto the city of Washington.

11. And he abode there many months, and he gave advice to Abraham, and to William, and sought to overthrow Tennessee and the South.

12. Now the men of the South was angry with Andrew, and they cursed him in their hearts, and sought an opportunity to slay him.

13. And there was a man who dwelt in East

Tennessee, in the city of Knoxville, and his name was William, and his surname was Brownlow.

14. And William was a prophet after the order of the Methodists, and he prophesied in all the regions round about Knoxville.

15. He had flocks, and herds, and cattle, and men-servants, and maid-servants.

16. Moreover, he was the editor of a paper called the "Knoxville Whig." He was a man valorous in speech, insomuch that he was called a "Fire-eater," which, being interpreted, means, "the fighting parson."

17. And he took the part of Andrew, and joined himself to Abraham and his party, and became an enemy to the South.

18. Then the men of the South took him and cast him into prison, and they pulled down his house, and spoiled his printing-office.

19. And William lifted up his voice and said unto them, Spare my life, I pray you.

20. Inasmuch as they did not wish to have blood upon their hands, they spared his life;

21. And they sent him to Abraham and William, and he abode at Washington.

CHAPTER XVI.

EMERSON ETHRIDGE.

1. AMONG those who had been chosen from the tribe of Tennessee, as wise men to the great Sanhedrim at Washington, was Emerson, surnamed the eloquent.

2. He dwelt in the town of Dresden, in West Tennessee, to the north of the Obian river.

3. Now Emerson was a mighty man. His speech was not as the words of man, but as of an angel. His words were sweeter than the honey and the honey comb.

4. The people loved Emerson, and when he went forth, they spread flowers in his path, and knelt down in his presence.

5. Now it came to pass that Emerson was at the great city of Washington and saw Abraham;

6. And Abraham knew Emerson; and he knew that he was mighty and eloquent; and Abraham lifted up his voice and said,

7. "Emerson!" And Emerson said, speak Lord, for thy servant heareth.

8. And Abraham said, "Lo, the people of the South do rebel, even thy constituents: and they are this day preparing for war.

9. I have thought of thee, O Emerson. I have seen thee in visions of the night, and in the day have I meditated upon thee.

10. Now thou mayest be of great use unto me, O Emerson, and if thou wilt do as I bid thee, behold I will clothe thee in purple, and give thee much gold, and when peace is made, I will reward thee with a great Federal office."

11. And Emerson opened his mouth and said unto Abraham: Behold thy servant is before thee, my Lord, thou hast but to command, and he will do whatsoever thou sayest.

12. And Abraham said, Then, if I have found favor in thine eyes, do thou go into the Sanhedrim, and make a speech against Secession, and cause it to be printed, and send it in all West Tennessee;

13. And I will speak to Andrew, and ask him to make a speech, and to send it to East Tennessee, per-

adventure, that Tennessee will hearken unto you and unto Andrew, and flee from the wrath to come.

14. Then went Emerson to the great Sanhedrim, and he stood up in the midst of the elders, and made a speech against Secession.

15. And he caused it to be printed, and sent thousands of copies to Tennessee.

16. But when it was come to Tennessee, and the people read it, then was their wrath kindled against Emerson.

17. And they said one to another, Emerson hath betrayed us. He is not our friend, but our enemy; even now he taketh part with the Black Republicans.

18. And they sent a message unto him, saying, Come thou not near us; for thou art a traitor, and if thou come unto us, we will hang thee, as thou deservest.

19. Then was Emerson sore afraid, and he went unto Abraham, and laid the matter before him, and concealed nothing.

20. And Abraham spake kindly unto him, and bade him remain in his house.

21. And Emerson abode with him many days.

CHAPTER XVII.

BATTLE OF BELMONT.

1. At the beginning of this War, Abraham had stationed troops at Cairo, and Ulysses, whose surname is Grant, had command of them.

2. Now, Leonidas, whose surname is Polk, who was in times past, Bishop of Louisiana, was stationed at Columbus, at the distance of eight leagues from Cairo.

3. And Leonidas had fortified Columbus by building a great wall, and digging a deep ditch, and he had placed upon the wall, many great guns and engines of war.

4. And Ulysses was greatly desirous of seizing Columbus, and taking Leonidas and all his men captives;

5. So he took a strong force, and embarked in boats, and descended the river until Columbus was in sight.

6. Then he caused the boats to stop, and his men went out upon the dry land, on the west side of the river, even upon the Missouri shore, and marched down upon the brink of the river.

7. But Leonidas was a cunning man; for he had sent spies to bring him word of the movements of Ulysses, and he had sent one legion across the river to meet Ulysses.

8. And when it was told him, that Ulysses was coming with a great force, he sent a great army over to meet him;

9. And the two armies met, and a great battle was fought, and the ground was covered with dead men.

10. And the blood flowed in streams, for the carnage was very great.

11. Many were the widows and orphans that were made that day. Many brave men went forth into that deadly contest, to return no more.

12. They sleep in silence upon the battle-marked plains of Belmont, and dream of war no more.

13. When Ulysses saw that Leonidas had so many men, and had so strongly fortified the town, he called off his men, and they returned to Cairo.

CHAPTER XVIII.

BOSS HALE.

1. Now it came to pass during the days of the Rebellion, when Tennessee had seceded, and united herself with Jefferson and the Southern Confederacy,

2. That there dwelt in the Western part thereof, even in the county of Gibson, and on the bank of the Forked Deer river, a certain widow, and her name was Jurene, but her surname was Hale.

3. And her house was in the midst of a great plain, and about two leagues from the city of Humboldt.

4. And Jurene had a large plantation, and orchards that were fruitful, and meadows that brought forth clover, and fields of corn, and wheat, and oats, and barley.

5. Moreover, she had patches of rye, and onions, and turnips.

6. And Jurene had man-servants and maid-servants,

and cows and oxen, and mules and asses and she-asses, and goats and many sheep.

7. And Jurene sold much of the produce of her farm at Humboldt and at Memphis, and made great gain.

8. And she was a good woman, for she fed the poor, and visited the sick, and gave aid to the orphan.

9. And she feared God and paid the preachers, and often invited them home to dine at her house.

10. And all that knew Jurene loved her.

11. And Jurene had several sons, and they had grown to be young men, and they were sprightly and active in business, and lived with ther mother, and cultivated her grounds.

12. And it came to pass when the Rebellion came, Jurene was troubled in mind, for she was opposed to war and loved peace.

13. And when Jefferson called upon the young men of the South, to join the Confederate army, Jurene's eldest son and the second eldest, joined the Southern army.

14. Then was Jurene vexed in spirit, for she said, if they slay my sons what good will my life do me?

15. And her third son was named Boss, and he was a mere lad, not having attained the stature of a man.

16. And Boss was fair and comely to look upon, and his eyes were blue, and his hair hung down upon his shoulders, in black and waving ringlets.

17. And Boss had been to school, and had learned to read and write; moreover, he had learned English Grammar and Robinson's Arithmetic, and Algebra as far as Equations of the second degree.

18. And the neighbors all loved Boss, for he was kindly disposed and moral, and they always bade him welcome to their houses.

19. And the maidens loved Boss because he was handsome and young, and moral and industrious, and seemed likely at no distant day, to make some one of them intensely happy.

20. And when James and Nathaniel, his two elder brothers, joined the army, they left Boss at home, that he might see to his mother's affairs.

21. Now it came to pass that the army was at a place called Union City, in West Tennessee, and Frank, whose surname was Cheatham, was in command thereof.

22. And Frank was willing to do the people a pleasure, so he commanded those having charge of the cars to give a grand excursion to the people on a certain day, that they might come and see him review the Tennessee Militia, at Union City.

23. And thousands of the people both men and women, went on the cars, and saw the great review.

24. And the soldiers gave a great party, and they spread wheat bran upon the ground, and they danced with the maidens that came to see them.

25. And the people brought them many delicacies from home, such as honey, parched corn, dried beef, roast turkey, and fresh butter.

26. And when the time had come to go on this great excursion to see the soldiers, Jurene arose, and took Boss with her, and went to see her two sons.

27. And when Boss had seen the army, and the uniform of the officers, and the evolutions of the soldiers, he greatly desired to become a soldier.

28. And he communed with his brothers, and expressed his desire to them;

29. But they said unto him, "Go away home with our mother, and stay with her and feed her flocks, and

water her mules; for thou art but a lad, and not a man of war."

30. Then was the young lad vexed, and his soul was stirred within him, for he longed to be a Confederate soldier.

31. And he ceased not day and night to importune his mother.

32. And when she could no longer pacify him, she promised that he might go when the corn was gathered into barns.

33. Then was Boss glad, and he fell to and wrought with great zeal until the last nubbin was cribbed.

34. Then he arose and went to Columbus, and joined the rebels under Gen. Polk.

35. And it came to pass on the next day, General Grant came with a great army, and Gen. Polk went out to meet him, and the battle of Belmont was fought;

36. And Boss fell down upon the battle field and lay among the dead;

37. And at night he was carried to the camp, wrapped in his blanket, but he was cold and dead.

38. And on the third day, they laid his dead body on the cars, and he was taken home to his mother.

39. When the youths and maidens came together to see poor Boss, and they fell upon his pale face and wept, and they refused to be comforted.

40. And on the morrow they buried Boss, and they have planted willows upon his grave and taught them to weep.

41. Oh! that men would cease to love war, and that they would learn to dwell in peace.

CHAPTER XIX.

GENERAL M'CLELLAN.

1. When Winfield, the great chief, saw that he had not won the victory at Manassas, he was sore vexed, and he communed with Abraham;

2. And he said unto Abraham, Lo! I am an old man, and have fought many battles, and never lost one before. And he wept bitterly.

3. But Abraham comforted him, and spake kindly to him, and gave him a taste of champaigne, and a little honey, and his soul revived.

4. And he lifted up his voice and said, "Abraham."

5. And Abraham said unto him, speak on.

6. And Winfield told Abraham that he was too old and infirm to undergo the fatigues of a campaign, or to command so great an army.

7. And he expressed a desire to resign the chief command of the army, that Abraham might appoint

another, younger, and more able to perform the service demanded.

8. And Abraham chose George, whose surname is McClellan, but in the fashionable lingo of the day, he is styled "The young Napoleon."

9. And George became the Commander-in-Chief of all the United States forces.

10. And George was a man skilled in war, and valiant. He had been to Europe, and learned many things that were useful to him as a great General.

11. And all the people loved George, and the soldiers had great confidence in him.

12. But the time would fail us to speak of all the exploits and battles of George.

13. For he fought many great battles with Lee, the Confederate General, and sought to circumvent him;

14. But Gen. Lee is a cunning man, and no man has ever circumvented him, and Gen. McClellan failed to take Richmond.

15. And behold! after many months Richmond was not still taken, but remained the capital of the Confederacy;

16. And the thing vexed Abraham; and he swore

in his wrath, that George should be no longer Commander-in-Chief;

17. And he took away his command, and gave it to Gen. Halleck, who became Commander of all the armies of the United States.

18. And the people wondered why Abraham did this thing, for as to George, they could find no fault in him.

19. And there were many other Generals, whom the time will not permit us to dwell upon.

20. Such was Gen. Pope, and Gen. Sickles, and Gen. Fremont, and Gen. Meade; and besides, an infinite number of Colonels and Majors.

CHAPTER XX.

FORT HENRY.

1. Now it is known to all the dwellers in the land, that there are two rivers that flow through Tennessee, toward the West;

2. The name of the first river is Tennessee, and the name of the second, is the Cumberland.

3. And these rivers flow through Kentucky, and empty their waters into the Ohio river above Cairo.

4. And behold the Confederates had built forts on these rivers, to keep the Federals from ascending.

5. The fort that the Confederates did build on the Cumberland, was called Fort Donelson, and it was eight furlongs from the city of Dover.

6. And the fort that was built on the Tennessee river, was called Fort Henry.

7. And Lloyd, whose surname is Tighlman, was

made Commander of that Fort, and he was a brave man, and skilled in building railroads.

8. And Lloyd collected many men in the fort, with provisions to last them many days, for he had heard that Ulysses was coming against him with a great army.

9. And there were in the fort very many spearmen, and a great number of archers and slingers, and of horsemen not a few.

10. And there were spies that went out by day, and others that went out by night, to see if Ulysses and his army were approaching.

11. And it came to pass that the spies looked down the river, and they beheld the gunboats, and they ran and told Lloyd, behold the Federals are approaching.

12. Then Lloyd commanded to blow the trumpet, and to assemble all his spearmen, and archers, and slingers, and mighty captains, and to prepare for battle.

13. And when the gunboats came near, the two armies joined battle, and they fought valiantly.

14. And the battle continued many days, and many were slain, and hundreds were covered with wounds,

15. Then Lloyd summoned his men of war, and took council of them. And Lloyd said, why should all these men be slain? Behold they are our friends and kindred, and we cannot fight longer against Ulysses, for he has more men than we.

16. And his majors, and captains, and lieutenants, counselled him to surrender, that his men might be saved alive.

17. And Lloyd surrendered, and he and all his men became prisoners of war, and were carried away to the North.

18. Then the gunboats kept on up the Tennessee river until they passed through the State of Tennessee, and came into Florence, which lies within the province of Alabama.

CHAPTER XXI.

FORT DONELSON.

1. Fort Donelson was built on the Cumberland river.

2. Now, the great city of Nashville, the capital of Tennessee, stands also on the Cumberland river, and it is at the distance of thirty leagues from Fort Donelson.

3. And the Confederates, who in the Yankee tongue, are called *Rebels*, said, let us make Fort Donelson very strong, lest the enemy come, and drive us away, and take the place, and advance upon Nashville.

4. And they built an exceeding high wall, with towers and parapets, for their archers and slingers, and they dug a ditch very deep.

5. Then said they one to another, we are safe in this fort, for the Yankees can never take us.

6. Now Jefferson had sent Gideon to command at

Fort Donelson, and Gideon had many legions with him;

7. And he had chosen men, who were mighty in battle, expert with the bow, and with the lance, and battle-axe.

8. When Ulysses had taken Fort Henry, he said, I will capture Fort Donelson also, then can I advance to Nashville, the great "city of Rocks."

9. And Ulysses made ready to go forth against Donelson. He had a very great army, so many were they in number, that no man could count them;

10. And he had gunboats and transports, and mighty guns, and battering rams, and other engines of war.

11. And he ascended the Cumberland river, and when he had drawn nigh to Fort Donelson, he caused the boats to halt, and some of his men he sent out on the land, and some remained on the boats.

12. And he prepared to attack Gideon on all sides, both by land and water.

13. And they joined battle, and there was great slaughter, for many of the forces of Ulysses fell, and many rebels also fell in battle.

14. And the battle lasted until the going down of the sun, and neither side would yield.

15. And on the morrow, at the early dawn, the battle was renewed, and it raged all that day, for the men were valiant on both sides.

16. And when the sun was set the battle ceased, but the scene was mournful to behold, for the dead lay over all the ground, and the blood of the slain ran in rivulets.

17. When darkness covered the land, then communed Gideon with his men of war, and his two chiefs, Buckner and Floyd, counseled him to sue for peace, lest the men should all perish.

18. But Gideon would not sue for peace, saying that he would not come alive into the hands of Ulysses.

19. Then Buckner the chief, a man of great discretion and valor, said, I pray thee, O Gideon, that thou wouldst hear me in behalf of my men.

20. And Gideon beckoned to him with his hand, to speak on.

21. And Buckner said, it is known to all here

present, that I entreated the people of Kentucky, to engage in this war, and they consented, and joined my legion, and gave me their young men and their sons.

22. And these are now with me, and they are good men and brave. Now, if battle be waged again to-morrow, these must perish by the sword;

23. For Ulysses is receiving fresh troops every hour, and he has already as many men as we, so that we cannot resist him.

24. But, if we will surrender, then will Ulysses spare the lives of the men.

25. Then Gideon lifted up his voice and said, I have vowed never to surrender to a Yankee; but as to thyself and those under thy command, thou art permitted to do as seemeth good in thy sight.

26. And Gideon and some of his chief Captains arose a great while before day, and escaped from Fort Donelson, and fled to Nashville.

27. And when it was day, Gen. Buckner sent a flag of truce to Ulysses, and asked a conference.

28. And Ulysses held a conference with him, and received his army in surrender.

29. And the number of prisoners which Ulysses received was very great. And Fort Donelson with its munitions of war and great guns came into the hands of Ulysses and the Federals.

CHAPTER XXII.

SURRENDER OF NASHVILLE.

1. Now, when it was noised abroad at Nashville, that Donelson had fallen, there was no small stir among the people;

2. For they said, our city must fall into the hands of the enemy. And many of them arose and fled from the city.

3. And there was one Sydney, a man of war, among the Confederates, and he was a General, and had a great army with him, and had been stationed at Bowling Green many months.

4. But when Sydney knew that Fort Donelson had fallen into the hands of Ulysses, he said, we must get hence, or the Federals will bag us all.

5. And he fled with his army and passed through Nashville, and destroyed bridges, and spread great alarm throughout all the land.

6. Then came certain messengers to Ulysses, from Abraham, saying, go thou up the Tennessee river, and drive away that haughty rebel Braxton, whose surname is Bragg.

7. For Braxton had joined himself to Beauregard, and they had a great army at Corinth.

8. And Abraham sent *Buell*, a very gallant chief, with a great army, to seize Nashville, the capital of Tennessee.

9. And when he was yet a great way off from the city, messengers came to the city, saying that they would surrender the city into his hands, without any bloodshed.

10. And the Federals marched into Nashville and took possession thereof, and found there much bread, and stores of meat, and arms without number, which the rebels could not carry with them.

11. And Isham, the Governor of Tennessee fled from Nashville, and carried with him the parchments, and the sacred books, and all the silver and gold he could find.

12. And he came unto Memphis, and told the people there what things had befallen Nashville.

13. And the people of Memphis were sore vexed, and they rent their clothes, and sat in sackcloth and ashes, and refused to be comforted.

14. For they feared that the same destiny was awaiting their own city.

CHAPTER XXIII.

BATTLE OF SHILOH.

1. And it came to pass after Ulysses had taken Fort Donelson, that he ascended the Tennessee river, determined to fight a great battle with Beauregard and Bragg.

2. Now, these rebel chiefs had collected a mighty army at Corinth, which is a town in the tribe of Mississippi, in the Northern part thereof.

3. Two great roads of iron had been made to cross at this place, and, besides, Corinth is about six leagues to the South of Pittsburg Landing, a place on the Tennessee river.

4. Ulysses directed his gunboats, and iron-clads, and transports to Pittsburg Landing, and soon his vast army had arrived at that place.

5. Now, Buell, the great Federal Chief, after he had captured Nashville, left a force there and marched

on to make further conquests; and when Ulysses had heard that Beauregard was at Corinth with a great army,

6. He sent word to Gen. Buell to come and join himself unto him, to give Beauregard battle with their united forces.

7. And certain came to Beauregard, and told him this, and he determined to give Ulysses battle without delay, before the other General could come unto him.

8. And it was in the month of April, and in the early part thereof, about the time the birds do choose their mates, and the flowers in the balmy South do burst forth into beauty and loveliness, that these things came to pass.

9. And Beauregard, in the self-same month, and on the sixth day thereof, at the dawn of day marched forth his legions, and gave the sign of battle.

10. And Ulysses went forth to meet him, and a mighty battle commenced; for they had great engines of war, and battering rams.

11. And the battle raged with great fury; for it seemed as if the solid earth would rend assunder, and the elements above had come in collision.

12. Never since men first began to dwell upon the face of the earth, had any seen the like, man slaying his fellow-man, and even one brother slaying another.

13. The earth was drenched in human gore, and the blood ran in rivulets, and the dead lay in heaps over all the land.

14. And the battle continued all the day even until the going down of the sun.

15. And when the night was come, and it was dark, the voice of lamentation, mingled with groans, was heard; for there were many wounded and dying.

16. Many are the orphans and widows that were made such on that day; for many fathers and husbands, as well as brothers and sons, were fated to gladden the social circle with their presence no more.

17. O that men would cease to study the rude arts of war, and that the nations might be at peace.

CHAPTER XXIV.

BATTLE OF SHILOH.—(CONTINUED.)

1. Now it came to pass when it was night, Gen. Buell was come with his legions, and Ulysses greeted him kindly.

2. And when the day dawned they united their forces, and the battle again commenced.

3. And the rebels were brave and determined, and fought till the second hour in the evening.

4. But the Federals were so many, and they were brave, so that they pressed upon the rebels greatly.

5. And they slew Sydney, whose surname is Johnson, one of the chiefs of the rebels.

6. And when the rebels knew that Sydney, their chief, was dead, they were greatly dejected, and began to retreat.

7. Then Ulysses commanded his men to pursue

them retreating, and they pursued them, and slew great numbers of them.

8. And when the sun was down, the rebels were all gone from the battle field save the dead and wounded, and Ulysses had gained a great victory.

9. But many were slain on both sides, and very many were led away captives.

10. And Ulysses remained many days at Pittsburg Landing, and buried the dead, and gave aid to those who had received wounds.

11. Meanwhile Beauregard and Braxton were at Corinth, and they made great fortifications there, and awaited the coming of Ulysses.

12. And after some days, Ulysses marched his army toward the South, and pitched his camps hard by the outer walls of the rebel fortifications.

13. And many were the skirmishes that took place, and many were the men who fell in them.

14. For neither Braxton nor Ulysses would make a general attack, but sought to find some advantage.

15. And the Federals sent great reinforcements to Ulysses, and he began to besiege Corinth.

16. When Braxton and Beauregard had perceived

this, they marched forth quietly by night, and withdrew toward the South.

17. And Ulysses did not know that the rebels were retreating until they were all gone.

18. And he was sore vexed because of this thing.

CHAPTER XXV.

CAPTURE OF NEW ORLEANS.

1. New Orleans was a mighty city. It stood on the coast of the great river, even the Mississippi, not far from the sea.

2. The merchants of New Orleans were as princes, for they dwelt in houses built of stone and marble, ornamented with brass, and gold, and silver, and precious stones.

3. And ships came to the city from all parts of the world, bringing corn, and wine, and silk, and all costly merchandize.

4. And the people of the city were cunning in all kinds of work, such as carving in stone, and iron, and brass. And they made books, and images, and garments, and sent them into all the parts of the earth.

5. And people of all languages, from all the tribes,

and kindreds upon the face of the whole earth, came unto the city.

6. And there were the mighty ships that came across the deep and wide sea, and the great steamboats that ply the Mississippi river, and the stern wheelers that paddle along the smaller rivers, and innumerable flat-boats from up the country.

7. And no city in the world, was equal unto it for cotton; for it came down the great river, and down the Arkansas, and Red River.

8. And ships came from England, and France, and from all parts of the world, to carry cotton away with them.

9. And the city was filled with oranges, and figs, and pomegranates, and peá-cans, and ginger, and spice, and parched corn.

10. Now, when the other Southern States seceded, Louisiana seceded also, and New Orleans was rank for secession.

11. And when the war began, it sent to Jefferson, a thousand pounds weight of gold, and a ton of silver, and darts and javelins without number.

12. And certain messengers went from the city to

Jefferson saying, Live, forever! O Jefferson; thou hast but to command, and we will every man obey!

13. Then were forts built upon the river below New Orleans, to keep the Federal gunboats away from the city.

14. And mighty guns and huge mortars were mounted, and many men were put in the forts.

15. Now runners came to Abraham, and knelt down in his presence, and told him of all these things.

16. Then was Abraham's wrath kindled, and he sent his armies to go by way of the sea, and to pull down the forts that the rebels had built, and to capture the great city.

17. And there was great commotion among the people, for they knew that the rebels would fight, and that there would be great carnage.

18. And Abraham's ships and gunboats being filled with armed men, and great guns, and swords, and spears, ascended the great river;

19. And when they were come to the forts, the rebels fired upon them, and they fired upon the rebels, and there was a great battle.

20. And many of the Federals and of the rebels were slain, and there was much bloodshed.

21. And the contest lasted many days, but the strength of the rebels began to fail.

22. Then did the Federals press more vehemently, and they beat down the forts, and burnt all the towers, and captured all the men that were within.

23. And the gunboats passed up the river, even to the city, and demanded that the whole city of New Orleans, surnamed the "Crescent City," be surrendered to the Federals.

24. And the city was surrendered, and all its stores, and treasures of gold and silver, and wine, and costly drink, and cups of gold, and curious vessels of wood, and stone, and brass, came into the hands of the Federals.

25. And Abraham sent General Butler to rule over the city

26. And Gen. Butler set up flags with the Stars and Stripes in the markets and public places, and commanded that all the men in the city, should reverence the flag.

27. Now, there were some there that hated Abraham and the old flag, and they would not reverence the flag.

28. Then sent the commanding General and seized these disobedient citizens, and spoiled their houses, and cast them into prison.

CHAPTER XXVI.

EVACUATION OF COLUMBUS.

1. WHEN Leonidas whose surname was Polk, heard that Fort Henry was taken, he was sore vexed.

2. And he rent his clothes, and put ashes on his head, and smashed his brandy demi-john.

3. And he would take no meat, but was in much trouble.

4. For he was in fear that Ulysses would come against him, and cast him into outer darkness.

5. Then he called a council of war. And when his Brigadiers, and Adjutants, and Colonels, and all the shoulder-strappers came unto his tent,

6. He showed them how much he loved Jefferson, and how much he hated Abraham;

7. Moreover, he told them that Fort Henry had fallen, and that the Federals were planning to fall upon Columbus, and utterly demolish it.

8. Then great fear fell upon the Council, and they looked one upon another in great consternation.

9. And certain spake unto Leonidas, and said, would it not be well, O most excellent Leonidas, to pull up stakes and leave these diggins immediately, if not sooner?

10. And Leonidas gave his consent, and he commanded to sound the trumpet, and when the army was drawn up, he commanded the chief musician to play a tune called in the Yankee tongue, "The Grand Skeedaddle."

11. And while the melody of this Southern favorite was filling the air, the great army of Leonidas, with all the spearmen, and archers, and sharp-shooters, and engineers, and drummers, arose and marched away from Columbus, and took their course toward the land of "Dixie."

12. Now it is known to all the dwellers in these parts, that there is an Island on the Mississippi river, below Columbus, called "Island No. 10."

13. And the water ran on this side of the island and on that,—on the right hand and on the left.

14. When Leonidas saw the Island, he sent men to

build a garrison there, long before he left Columbus; for, he said, lest Columbus may fall into the enemy's hands.

15. And the Island was fortified, and a great force was placed there;

16. And Leonidas sent to all that lived down the river, greeting, saying, Fear not, for Island No. 10 cannot fall.

17. Then the people said one to another, behold we are safe, for Leonidas is a man of truth.

18. But when Leonidas left Columbus and traveled toward Dixie, great fear seized the people.

19. And the Federals came and took possession of Columbus, and prepared to move against Island No. 10.

20. And they descended the river and they cannonaded the fort on the Island, and beseiged it, and the seige lasted many weeks.

21. And the two forces threw shells at each other, and made much noise.

22. And the Federals took Island No. 10, and all its men they made prisoners of war, and they carried

away all its stores of meat and flour, and powder and ball.

23. Then great fear came upon all the dwellers in West Tennessee and North Mississippi, for they said, behold the Yankees will come hither also.

CHAPTER XXVII.

FALL OF FORT PILLOW AND CAPTURE OF MEMPHIS.

1. Leonidas had fortified a place on the river, below Island No. 10, on the Tennessee shore, and had called it Fort Pillow.

2. And Fort Pillow was made of vast strength so as to withstand a mighty force.

3. And Leonidas had sent into all the regions round about, commanding all to send their negro men to Fort Pillow, to work on the fortifications.

4. Then were the sable sons of Ham gathered together by twenties, and by fifties, and by hundreds, carrying pickaxes and spades, and marching to Fort Pillow.

5. And they came to the fort and digged a mighty ditch, for it was deep and wide; and they built a high wall, and set up a tower.

6. And they put up their largest guns, and made ready to fight the Federals.

7. But the Federals said, Wherefore shall we be discouraged? Have we not taken divers forts? Has not Fort Henry and also Fort Donelson fallen before us?

8. And Island No. 10, behold it could not stand before us. Shall we fear to attack Fort Pillow.

9. And they arose and marched against Fort Pillow, and threw shells at it.

10. And the rebels threw shells at the Federals, and there was strife between them many days.

11. Then certain of the rebels said, why should we stay here, and suffer these uncircumcised Yankees to lead us away into captivity, to make us hewers of wood and drawers of water?

12. For we cannot withstand them,—they are more numerous than we.

13. Let us arise by night and get away into the land of Dixie, that we may not come alive into the hands of our enemy.

14. Then the rebels rose up a great while before day,

when it was yet dark, and spiked their great guns, and spoiled all their goods, and fled from Fort Pillow.

15. And when the morning was come, and the Federals looked toward the Fort, behold it was empty, for the rebels had fled.

16. Then went forth a mighty rumor, behold Fort Pillow hath fallen into the hands of the Federals.

17. And the people were alarmed, and many of them arose and fled from their homes, and went far South into the land of Dixie.

18. And the Federals collected their gunboats, and their men, and made ready to go down the river to Memphis, and take the city.

19. And it was on the sixth day of June, in the second year of the reign of Abraham, that they came against Memphis.

20. And when they had come in sight of the city, they fired their cannon, and marched against it.

21. And the rebels that were on their gunboats before the city, moved out to meet the Federals, and a battle was fought between them.

22. But the Federal powers prevailed, and some of

the rebel gunboats they sunk, and some they took captive.

23. And the fleet of the rebels was dispersed, and the Federals took the city, and hoisted the "Stars and Stripes" on the Post Office.

24. And the mayor and other chief men of the city, made friends with the Federals, and they entered into covenant with them.

25. But many were they who fled from the city, and left their homes and all their household stuff, that they might not come alive into the hands of the Federals.

CHAPTER XXVIII.

FEDERAL DOMINION IN MEMPHIS.

1. Now it has been written in these Chronicles, that the Federals had troops at Cairo, and they would not permit any steamboats to come down the river to Memphis.

2. And, as the people South, do not cultivate the land for much corn or wheat, but for cotton, when supplies came not down the river, the prices became exceeding high, so that no poor man could buy.

3. And many began to be in want. And there were speculators in those days, men who did not have the fear of God before them, and cared for nothing but old Bourbon and money.

4. And these speculators bought up all the corn and meat, and wine, and flour, and corn meal, and sold them at a five-fold price to those who had money to buy.

5. Now, hunger began to press upon the poorer classes, and those whose business the war had destroyed or injured, and their wives and little ones had no bread;

6. But when the Federals had taken the city, boats from Cincinnati, and from Louisville, and from the "Sucker" State, came down the river, and brought provisions for man and beast.

7. And when the people beheld that the stock of provisions was better, and the price cheaper than when the rebels held the city, they were contented, and bade the Federals welcome.

8. And the Federals put a guard of armed men around the city, and would not let any one pass out of the city, unless he would swear to keep a covenant with Abraham and all Union men.

9. Nor would they allow any one to carry out of the city any goods, lest, peradventure, the rebels should receive comfort and aid therefrom.

10. Then was the price of cotton very high, for it was scarce, inasmuch, as the rebels had burnt all the cotton.

CHAPTER XXIX.

GEORGE DRURY AND ELLEN GRAINGER.

1. About the time that James, whose surname is Buchanan, was the embodiment of Uncle Samuel, which (being interpreted) was President of the United States,

2. There dwelt a family named Grainger, in the great State of Pennsylvania.

3. And the family consisted of a mother, who was a widow, a son whose name was Lindley, and two daughters, named Susan and Ellen, and they were all grown.

4. And they were poor, because the mother owned but a small farm, and a few cattle, and a neat cottage.

5. But Lindley was well educated and intelligent, and his sisters were skilled in the arts and sciences, and Ellen, the younger, handled the harp and played

upon the piano, and was fair and beautiful to look upon.

6. Now, Susan and Ellen said "let us teach school, and bring in some aid to our brother in supporting ourselves and our mother."

7. And they taught a small school and were pleased with the business of instruction, and their students loved them.

8. And it came to pass that a stranger passed that way, and he was from the South country, even from the province of Alabama;

9. And when he saw the two young girls, and had heard the people speak so much in their praise,

10. He said to them, what compensation do these people give you for your services to their children?

11. And Susan, the elder, said, they pay us the sum of twenty dollars each per month.

12. And the stranger said, if you will arise, and come to Alabama, then will the people give you fifty dollars a month. And he encouraged Susan and Ellen to go South.

13. And when he had returned home, he spake to

his neighbors of Susan and Ellen, and the people made them a school.

14. And the stranger wrote to the two girls, and they packed up their trunks, and went to Alabama;

15. And they took a school and the people loved Susan and Ellen; because they were kind and attentive to their children, and taught them with great care.

16. Now, there dwelt hard by their school-house, a rich cotton planter, whose name was George, but his surname was Drury. And George was five and twenty years of age, and possessed a manly form and a goodly countenance.

17. And he had a large estate, and a hundred slaves, and lived in a great house, made of brick, and he had never been married;

18. And when George saw Ellen, and heard all the neighbors speak in her favor, he loved her;

19. And he went to the house in which she boarded, and talked with her, and she played on the piano, and sung songs to his great delectation.

20. And George dreamed every night of Ellen's

soft blue eyes, and her little delicate hands, and the music of her sweet young voice;

21. And George was restless by day when at home, for he said, *it is not good for me to be alone.*

22. And George was in love with Ellen, and he said unto her "O Ellen, live forever!"

23. Moreover, he said, "Why shouldst thou toil through winter's cold and summer's heat to obtain a living? For behold I have enough for thee and me,

24. "Arise, Ellen, thou loved one, and come to my house, and become my wife, and thou shalt have white bread and fresh butter, and live on the cream of the South."

25. And the saying pleased Ellen, and she lifted up her voice and said "Amen!"

CHAPTER XXX.

GEORGE AND ELLEN.—(CONTINUED.)

1. And it came to pass, that Ellen communed with Susan and told her what George had proposed to her.

2. And Susan replied to Ellen, the thing is good, for George is a just man, and he will be to thee a kind husband;

3. And Susan said further to her sister, behold we are away from our mother, and from our brother, and we are strangers in the sunny South;

4. Now, that we may test the love that George professeth for thee, say unto him, I cannot wed thee away from my mother's house, but if thou wilt wait until our session closes, and will then come to Pennsylvania, then will I be wedded to thee in the presence of my mother, and we will receive her blessing.

5. For she said to herself, if George hath much love

for me, he will not hesitate to make the trip and incur the expense, for he is a man of large means.

6. And when she had said these words to George, his love for her was increased a thousand fold, and he told her that he would be willing to follow her to the remotest verge of the green earth.

7. Then did they contract a marriage, and gave to each other the solemn pledge of fidelity, and they called upon the sweet little stars that were watching them from Heaven's canopy, to witness their plighted love.

8. And Time's chariot, whose wheels have never missed a revolution since creation was born, rolled on, and the session was near its close.

9. And Susan and Ellen wrote letters to their mother and brother, and they breathed the spirit of hope and love;

10. Then did the mother of these two girls and their lone brother rejoice at the prospect of receiving them to their home again.

11. Now, about this time Abraham's Proclamation calling for seventy-five thousand spearmen, was sent abroad, and war between the North and the South was about to commence.

12. Then came a despatch to Susan and Ellen from their mother, requesting them to hasten home lest they should be overtaken by the calamities of the war in the South;

13. And Ellen sent for George and communed with him; and George told her that a call was made upon the young men of Alabama, to go forth against the force of Abraham, and to fight for the South,

14. And that he had volunteered and had been elected Captain of a company;

15. And it was agreed between them, that their wedding should be postponed until the close of the war.

16. Then did they exchange ambrotypes, and renew their pledges of love and constancy, and the hour of separation came, and they separated to meet no more until the earthquake of war should have convulsed our once happy country.

17. And Susan and Ellen hastened away to their native State, and to their mother, and they found the people greatly agitated because of the war;

18. And their brother Lindley had volunteered, and he was elected Captain.

19. And the sisters were diligent in preparing clothes and equipments for their soldier brother.

20. Now it was in the first year of the reign of Abraham, and in the month of July, and on the twenty-first day of the self-same month, that a great battle was fought at Manassas;

21. And many were the dead, and the blood flowed in rivulets, and the slain were spread over a great extent of surface;

22. And on the morrow, George walked over the field of battle, and looked upon the fallen slain, and they were the slain of Abraham's forces.

23. And among them he saw a goodly young man, whose sword was yet held in his hand, now cold in death;

24. And his features bore evidence of the goodness of his heart.

25. And as George looked down upon him, he said, how cruel is war! this is a war of brothers,—it is unnatural, unchristian, and will bring a lasting disgrace upon our people.

26. And he said to those who were with him, I would that I could take the body of this fallen Captain,

and send it to his friends; but this cannot be seeing I know not his name, nor who are his friends, nor where they live;

27. Then did George stoop down and loose the sash from the fallen foe, and it was new and beautifully wrought;

28. And when he had examined it the more closely, behold he found embroidered upon the sash, in beautiful letters of silk, the words, "*Lindley Grainger, embroidered by his sister, Ellen.*"

29. Then did George know that it was the body of his lover's brother, and he wept upon it.

30. And he went to Richmond and procured a metallic case, and put the body of Lindley therein, and sent it home to his mother and sisters to be interred with kindred dust.

CHAPTER XXXI.

COTTON BURNING.

1. Now it came to pass in those days when the Confederates saw that the "Yankees" would take Memphis,

2. They sent men into all the regions round about to burn all the cotton they could find.

3. And many people had their cotton in old houses, and desert places, and caverns, and in cellars.

4. And when Braxton, whose surname is Bragg, heard of this, his wrath was kindled, and sent a band of soldiers to cast all these people into prison, and to burn their houses, and destroy all their goods.

5. Then was there great distress, such as was never known in Dixie before: for the people had no corn, nor had they meat, nor coffee, nor sugar, and their supply of raiment was not a little scanty.

GREAT REBELLION. 125

6. And they murmured against Braxton and Jefferson, and were sore vexed.

7. And they sent messengers to Jefferson, saying, We pray thee protect us from cotton burning, for it is all we have left of our living.

8. For our young men are gone to war, and thy Generals have sent and taken away our guns and pistols, and left us no arms for defence,

9. And the Federals have come to Memphis, and offer us gold and silver for our cotton; let us, we pray thee, sell them a little cotton of this crop of 1862, that we may buy bread that our little ones may eat thereof and not die.

10. But Jefferson was wroth, and sent unto them saying, Whosoever shall sell a Yankee a pound of cotton, shall surely be put to death.

11. Now, there dwelt in the land of Mississippi, and in the Northern part thereof, a family named Byron;

12. And Mr. Byron was a man of moderate means, and his farm was small, but he was a good man and just, for he feared God, hated the devil, and would not touch ardent drink.

13. And Mr. Byron had two sons, who had attained

to manhood, and two daughters that were lovely maidens, and several smaller children.

14. Now, when the Rebellion broke out, and many cunning men and eloquent orators were urging the people to fight against the government of their fathers, these two sons of Mr. Byron joined the Confederate army, and were sent to Virginia.

15. And the elder of them died of a fever, and was buried in the soil of old Virginia far away from home and loved ones;

16. And the younger son was slain in the battle of Shiloh, and his father went to the battle ground to seek for him, but he could not find him;

17. And Mr. Byron was vexed in mind and broken hearted, and returned home in great despair;

18. And he fell sick of a fever and a broken heart, and died, and was buried in his own garden;

19. And as all their cotton for the former year had been burnt, and their few negroes, had fled to Memphis, they had nothing with which to purchase the necessaries of life;

20. And when the mother and the two girls saw

that the father and his two sons were dead, and there was none to labor for them,

21. They determined to raise some cotton: and they went out and labored in the fields, and with their soft, little, delicate hands, they handled the hoe, and did chop down the weeds, and dig about the roots of the cotton.

22. And the Lord blessed them, and sent them showers of rain, and their cotton grew, and became white in the patch.

23. And when it was autumn, they picked it out, and put it in bags, and then made ready to go to Memphis to sell it, and buy meat;

24. And the mother and her eldest daughter harnessed up their two horses, and put their cotton bags into the wagon, and drove on the road to Memphis;

25. Now, the distance was two score and two miles, and they drove on the way two days, and when they were only two miles away from the city, behold the guerillas came, and fell upon them, and burned up their cotton, and broke their wagon, and spoke harshly unto them.

26. And these women turned their footsteps homeward, sorrowing greatly because they had lost their cotton.

CHAPTER XXXII.

FEDERAL CONQUEST OF WEST TENNESSEE.

When General Grant had taken Memphis, he left a strong force in the city, and placed pickets all around it;

2. And he took with him many men, and marched into all the surrounding country, and seized upon all Confederates that he could find;

3. And his soldiers spread through all the country in West Tennessee and North Mississippi, and they took many horses, and mules, and much cattle, and corn and other valuables from such as sympathized with Jefferson and the South.

4. And they destroyed the railroads and burned down the bridges, and seized all the towns, and left soldiers at each to hold them in subjection.

5. And the Confederates were at Holly Springs,

which is a city of no mean repute, in North Mississippi, two score and ten miles from Memphis;

6. And Gen. Veatch went forth to capture them; and he led a mighty host with him, and they encamped upon the brink of a river, which is called "Cold Water;"

7. And the Confederates sent out spies, and they saw where Gen. Veatch was, with all his hosts;

8. They returned and brought word to those that sent them, and they were all alarmed, and arose and fled deeper down in "Dixie."

9. Then Gen. Veatch arose and marched his forces into Holly Springs, and seized upon it, and placed a garrison there.

10. Then were the Confederates at Tupola in Mississippi, and they gathered there from all points, Beauregard, and Bragg, and Polk, and many other rebels of high degree.

11. And when the summer had well-nigh passed away, Braxton, whose surname is Bragg, determined upon a grand stroke.

12. So he marched his men to Chattanooga, in East Tennessee, and thence north into Kentucky.

13. And when the people of Kentucky saw that the rebels were coming, they were greatly alarmed, and they sent all the men they could raise, to meet the invader and drive him off.

14. And they went forth to meet him, and they fought a great battle, and filled the country with mourning.

15. And the Federals claimed the victory, but the rebels said that they had the best of the fight.

16. And Gen. Bragg gave up the invasion of Kentucky, and marched back his mighty army into Middle Tennessee, and went into winter quarters near Murfreesboro.

17. And Gen. Sherman remained at Memphis, and he commanded that the guards should allow no one to pass out of the city, who had not taken an oath to support "Uncle Abe" and the North, against Jeff. Davis, and "the rest of mankind."

18. And many of the people were sore vexed, for they wished to come into Memphis, and to smuggle out goods to sell to the people in the South at enormous prices.

19. And there were Jay-hawkers in those days,

and they robbed men and women of their money, and silver-plate, and their horses and mules.

CHAPTER XXXIII.

CONTRABANDS.

1. And it came to pass in these days, that Abraham, whose surname is Lincoln, sent forth a proclamation into all the Provinces, States, Territories, Cities, and parts of the country,

2. Declaring that the negroes of all those who had taken up arms against the government, were free, and had a right to leave their masters;

3. Moreover, he commanded his Generals, and Captains of hundreds, and Captains of fifties, and all that were in command, and all soldiers, to protect such negroes as should runaway from their masters, and come to their lines.

4. Then did the sable sons of Ham, that had ever been in bondage, arise and leave their masters, and they fled to the Federal camps for protection.

5. And some of them took with them their wives

and little ones, and rejoicing in their freedom, they left the cotton fields and plantations of their masters.

6. And these were called contrabands.

7. And they collected at St. Louis, and Cairo, and Memphis, and Nashville, and at many other places, in thousands;

8. And they had no homes, and no money, and no friends, and they and their wives, and children began to be in want.

9. Then were the Federal commanders obliged to feed them; so they ordered rations to be dealt to them every day.

10. And still they continued to come from all parts of the South.

11. And the Abolitionists rejoiced because the negroes were made free, "for," said they, "the year of Jubilee is come."

12. And certain went unto the President saying, why not put all able-bodied negroes in the army, and cause them to fight against their masters and for their own freedom?

13. And the thing pleased Abraham, and he commanded them to put the United States uniform upon

the negroes, and to give them guns, and to teach them military tactics.

14. And when Jefferson heard these things, his wrath was kindled; and he said, as my soul liveth will I be revenged for this.

15. And he commanded his men, and all Confederates everywhere, and all "Secesh" throughout the South, to slay every negro found with arms against white men.

16. And the war progressed, and there were skirmishes and battles; and cities were plundered, and towns were burned, and the land was made to mourn because of the desolations of war.

17. And Jefferson and Abraham were bitter enemies one to the other, and they ceased not continually to vex each other.

CHAPTER XXXVI.

FAIR OAKS.—EFFORTS TO TAKE RICHMOND.

1. Now while George, who is also called Little Mac, was chief over the armies of Abraham, a great host was gathered together before Richmond, a walled city of the Confedrates.

2. And the people said, surely will terror seize upon the city, and trembling take possession of it;

3. Surely will the Rebels flee away, and Richmond be filled with emptiness.

4. Thorns shall spring up in her streets, and satyrs shall dance there; for the countenance of George will desolate the place.

5. Now the army of George was encamped upon the banks of a stream, the name of which is Chickahominy.

6. And a great storm arose insomuch that the Chickahominy was like unto a great river.

7. And while the soldiers did eat and drink in

their tents, there came a great body of Rebels from the Rebel camp, even from the camp of Lee.

8. Then began a great battle, and continued until the setting of the sun.

9. And the next day was the Sabbath day, and the Rebels came forth with a mighty host to overwhelm the Yankees.

10. But the hosts of George were brave, and they fell with great fury upon their enemies, and drove them back even at the point of the bayonet.

11. Four times did the Rebels fly before the bayonets of the North.

12. And many were killed, and many were sorely wounded upon the field.

13. And the name of the battle was called Fair Oaks, because of the trees that grow thereabout.

14. Now after many days had passed, the people clamored, saying, why hath not George taken the city, and why sitteth he idle in his tent.

15. And George's friends were wroth, and answering, said, ye civilians, ye are fools and know not military art. Hath not George wisdom, and is he not a great General even as Napoleon was great?

16. But when other many days had passed, Abraham grew restless and said unto George privily, My son, why goest thou not against these Richmondites?

17. George answered and said unto Abraham, wait. So Abraham waited.

18. Now while Abraham waited and George waited and the people waited, behold Lee waited not, but came forth from his strong places with a mighty army,

19. Gathered from all parts of Dixie and led by mighty men, even such as Jackson, and Hill, and Longstreet.

20. And when the month of June was well nigh ended, Lee's army fell upon the camp of George.

21. And on the twenty-seventh of the month, and on the day that is called Thursday, a battle was fought even from mid-day until the sun set.

22. That battle was called the battle of Mechanicsville, and in it many were slain, and the army of George fell back five miles.

23. When the sun rose on Friday, the battle was renewed. And the battle that day was called the battle of New Bridge, and great numbers were slain, and the army of George crossed the Chickahominy.

24. On the next day, which is called Saturday, many were slain, and the army of George retreated across the swamp which is called White Oak.

25. On the next day, which was the Sabbath day, were two mighty battles fought, and the army of George continued to retreat.

26. On Monday, which was the thirtieth, was another battle fought, and behold the army of George continued to retreat.

27. On Tuesday the fight continued until noonday even until the gunboats on the river, which is called James, put an end to the fight.

28. And George rested himself after his much fighting and much retreating, and behold Abraham cometh up to the camp and revieweth the troops.

29. And Abraham spake unto George, saying, My son, what wilt thou now do.

30. And George opened his mouth and gave answer saying, Oh, Abraham, if it seemeth good to thee, methinks I will wait a little while.

31. And Abraham laughed and said, verily thou puttest me in mind of a little anecdote.

CHAPTER XXXV.

HOLLY SPRINGS.

1. Now in those days, it came to pass that Holly Springs, in the tribe of Mississippi, had become a rebel stronghold.

2. Holly Springs was a goodly town in North Mississippi;

3. It was noted for its schools, and churches, and its stores of wine, and oil, and silk, and scarlet, and fine linen.

4. And the people had much gold and silver, and they dealt in cotton, and hemp, and flax, and lambs' wool, and young negroes.

5. And they believed in Jeff. Davis and the South, and ceased not day and night, to curse Lincoln and all the "Yankees."

6. And Gen. Van Dorn stationed a great army

there, and made fortifications, and a trench round the city.

7. And the people from all the regions round about, sent to him corn and provender for man and beast, and bade him God-speed.

8. And he sent into all the country, and collected corn, and fodder, and potatoes, and his men lived on the fat of the land.

9. And Gen. Villipegue joined himself to him, and brought all his forces to Holly Springs, and they made a covenant together to fight in the same cause.

10. When Gen. Grant, who was at Lagrange, with a host of Hoosiers, Suckers, Buckeyes, and Wolverines, heard of these things,

11. His wrath was kindled within him, and he determined to smite the rebels.

12. And he marched forth toward Holly Springs with a great army.

13. And when he was yet a great way off, certain Secesh spies came to Holly Springs, and told the rebel Generals, that the "Yankees" were coming.

14. Then did they pull up stakes and "skedaddle"

deeper down in Dixie, for they feared to meet Grant in deadly conflict.

15. And the people of Holly Springs were alarmed, seeing their protector was gone;

16. And they sat in sackcloth and ashes, and wept, and refused to be comforted;

17. For, said they, we will fall into the hands of these "Yankees," and they will slay us, and our wives, and little ones, and spoil our goods, and carry away our negroes.

18. And Gen. Grant marched into Holly Springs, and raised the Federal Flag, and caused the people to submit to the laws of Uncle Samuel.

19. Now all the rest of the acts of General Van Dorn and of General Villipegue, are they not written in the future chapters of these Chronicles?

20. And they led their men a great way from Holly Springs, and joined themselves to Sterling, whose surname is Price, a mighty man among the rebels.

CHAPTER XXXVI.

GEN. PRICE.

1. In those days when *Peace* reigned undisturbed, and *War* was a thing unknown in Columbia's happy land,

2. There dwelt a man in the land of Missouri, and his name was *Sterling*, surnamed Price;

3. And he was a just man, and feared God and kept His commandments.

4. Moreover, he was a man of great wisdom, and all the people loved him.

5. And he had been a ruler among them for many years, a judge, a member of the Legislature, and chief Magistrate of the Commonwealth.

6. Now, when the Rebellion broke out, he was living at home, as a man of peace.

7. And Claiborne, whose surname was Jackson, was at that time, Governor of Missouri;

8. And Claiborne knew Sterling, and he knew that the people loved him.

9. And he went unto Sterling and communed with him, and spake kindly unto him.

10. And he persuaded Sterling to join the fortunes of the South, and he made him a Major-General.

11. Then Sterling raised a large army to fight against the Union, and he was brave, and cared for his soldiers, and they loved him as dutiful sons would love an affectionate father.

12. And Sterling fought many battles, and became a great hero among the rebels.

13. But Jefferson was jealous of Sterling, and never confided in him, nor did he confer any great honor upon him.

14. And this vexed the people of Missouri, because they loved Sterling, and considered him the greatest man in all the Confederacy.

15. And Sterling marched his army Eastward and crossed the Mississippi river, and joined himself to Braxton, whose surname is Bragg.

16. And Sterling fought at Corinth and at other places, and all that knew him, both in the rebel, and

also in the Federal army, knew that no man was braver than Sterling, whose surname is Price, the ex-Governor of Missouri.

CHAPTER XXXVII.

THE GUERRILLAS.

1. When the Federal armies advanced into Dixie, all civil law was suspended;

2. Magistrates ceased to perform the functions of their offices, for no one could sue or be sued;

3. And there were no civil courts or criminal proceedings, and evil doers ceased to be afraid of the majesty of the law.

4. Then were there dishonest men that formed themselves into companies called Jayhawkers; and some companies they called Guerrillas;

5. And fearing neither God nor man, these men went through the land seizing upon cotton, and horses, and mules, and fat oxen, and money;

6. And they spared no one; nor cared they whether one was *Union* or *Secesh*, if he had money or other valuables, they demanded the same.

7. And they made the land to mourn because of their depredations; for they robbed thousands of families, and left them no means to procure bread for their little ones.

8. And the people near Memphis sent to General Veatch, and said, "Protect us, we pray thee, from these Jayhawkers, for they torment us day and night."

9. And General Veatch opened his mouth and said to them, "O generation of vipers, why do ye not come forward and take the oath of allegiance? How can I protect you while ye and your sons are in open rebellion against the government?

10. Repent ye, every one, and take the oath of allegiance to Uncle Samuel, then will I protect you and your little ones."

11. And these Guerrillas stopped the trains on the railroad, and robbed them, and burnt the cars;

12. And they burnt bridges, and tore up the track, and played "smash" generally.

13. And they collected on the Mississippi river, and erected batteries on the shore, and fired on steamboats, and made them "round to."

14. And they robbed them of their stores, and burnt the boats to the water's edge.

15. And this thing vexed the people, particularly the travelling public, and the steamboat men;

16. And they cried to General Hurlbut for relief.

17. And the General heard their prayer, and he sent forth his decree into all the world,

18. That whenever a steamboat was robbed, "ten" "Secesh" families should be banished from Memphis;

19. And whenever the Guerrillas should rob a railroad train, then the town or village of "Secesh" sympathizers nearest thereunto, should be burned to the ground.

20. Then were these Guerrillas afraid, but, nevertheless they did not altogether discontinue their robberies.

CHAPTER XXXVIII.

TAKING THE OATH.

1. Now it came to pass when Memphis was in the hands of the Federals, that James, whose surname is Veatch, was appointed to the command thereof.

2. And James gave commandment that no one should leave the city, or reside in the same, or carry on any business therein, unless he should take the oath of allegiance to Uncle Samuel.

3. And many of the good people murmured because of this order.

4. And they began to make excuses; for one of them said, I have two sons in the Confederate army; therefore, I pray thee have me excused.

5. And another came to James, and kneeling down, said unto him, my wife's father lives in the land of the South, and she expects to get a large lot of negroes at his death; therefore, I pray thee, have me excused.

6. And another came and said, "O James, whose surname is Veatch, most gladly would I obey thy every command: but the Southern Confederacy owes me a large sum of money, and, if I take the oath, they will never pay me; therefore, I pray thee, have me excused."

7. And still another came and said, "I have not at any time violated Uncle Samuel's laws, but I have kept them all inviolate; therefore, I pray thee, have me excused."

8. And yet another came and said unto James, "When the rebels were here, and they brought Federal prisoners from Belmont, I visited them in prison, and ministered unto them; and I fed the hungry, and gave a blanket to those that had none, and sung a song at the funeral of those that died; therefore, I pray thee, have me excused."

9. And yet another came, saying, "I own great possessions in Dixie, both of lands, and meadows, and orchards, and oxen, and horses;

10. Now, if I take the oath, Jefferson will confiscate all my property, and I shall be bereft of all my goods; therefore, I pray thee, have me excused."

11. And James was vexed because of their excuses, and his wrath was kindled. And James gave a commandment that no one should be excused, but that all should take the oath;

12. Moreover, he commanded, that if any refused to take the oath, his soldiers should spoil his house, and take his goods, and he should be cast into prison.

13. And guards were placed all around the city, to see that no one should leave the city, or carry out any goods, unless he would show a writing from James or his Provost-Marshal.

14. And James sent a guard into all parts of the city, and he commanded them to seize any that they might find drunk or disorderly, and cast them into prison.

15. And James established good order in the city.

CHAPTER XXXIX.

ADVENTURES OF TWO YOUNG SECESH.

1. And it came to pass in those days, when James, whose surname is Veatch, was in command of the Post of Memphis,

2. That many of the youths of that city, loved Jefferson and the South, and hated Lincoln and the Yankees.

3. And it grieved them sore to see the Federal soldiers, in Uncle Sam's uniform of blue, in all the streets, and upon all the corners, and at all places of the "Bluff City."

4. And they often spake against "Uncle Abe," and sent messages of love to some that were in the rebel army;

5. And they made the pictures of rebel flags on their slates at schools, and showed by many signs, that they did not choose "Uncle Abe" to rule over them.

6. Now, among these, were two; the name of one was *Harry*, and the name of the other was *Walter*.

7. And these had hardly come to the years of a man, but they were tall and of goodly size, and comely to look upon.

8. And their young Southern blood ran hot in their veins, at the thought, that the Yankees looked upon Tennessee and Memphis as being subdued;

9. And they went to the same school in the city, and sat on the same seat, and were very intimate;

10. And Walter was older than Harry, and nearer approached unto the stature of a man.

11. And when they were at school, Walter lifted up his voice, and said unto Harry, "My soul doth long to be in the rebel army."

12. And Harry answered and said, "And so doth mine,—that desire mingles with my dreams and with my waking thoughts, and I am dying to be away from school, and these hard lessons."

13. Then Walter said, "Let us arise and go and join ourselves unto the army of Bragg."

14. And the saying pleased Harry, and he gave his consent.

15. And they took each of them a horse and some script, and went forth beyond the city;

16. And when they had come to the pickets, seeing that they were only boys, they let them pass.

17. Then did these boys rejoice, for they felt that they were safe, and that they had escaped from school, and would no more have to get and recite hard lessons.

18. And they pursued their way for several days. And behold they lifted up their eyes and Federal cavalry were approaching;

19. And the cavalry overtook them, and captured them, and led them bound unto Fort Pillow.

20. And they took their horses from them, and sent them to Columbus, in the province of Kentucky, and put them in prison.

21. Then were these boys dejected in mind, for they could not join the army of Bragg, and they did not love the bean soup and cracker bread, that were given unto them in the prison.

22. And it repented them that they had not remained at home, and continued their lessons at school.

CHAPTER XL.

THE CONSCRIPTION.

1. Now it came to pass when the Federals had taken possession of all the province of West Tennessee, Middle Tennessee, North Alabama, and North Mississippi,

2. That Jefferson was alarmed, and he sent a message unto his wise men, who were assembled at the rebel Sanhedrim, at Richmond;

3. And he advised them to adopt powerful measures to drive the invaders from the "sacred soil" of the South;

4. Or, if they could not expel them from the territory already in their possession, that they should at least keep them from carrying the invasion any further.

5. And they communed one with another, saying, it is useless to call for any more volunteers;

6. For we have called so often, that the last one that is disposed to volunteer, is already in the army;

7. Then sent they to Jefferson, saying, we are sore vexed because we think no more men will volunteer; what is the commandment concerning this matter?

8. And Jefferson answered unto them, saying, there is but one measure which ye can adopt, which will save the country.

9. And they said unto him, "Speak on, O Jefferson!"

10. And Jefferson said, "If ye will pass a law calling every able-bodied man into the army, whether he will or not."

11. Then did the rebel Congress pass a law conscripting every man in the Southern Confederacy, between the ages of eighteen and forty-five.

12. And the thing vexed the people, for, said they, We have sent our sons, and our young men to the army, and we have remained at home to protect our wives and our little ones;

13. And now, if we go also into the army, who will there be to protect our home and loved ones?

14. And who will there be to cultivate our fields and vineyards for us?

15. And many of them said we will not obey this call of Jefferson and the rebel Congress, for we will not leave our homes and go to war.

16. And the rebel Generals sent recruiting officers into every part of the country, and they seized all that they could find, and compelled them to go into the army.

17. But many arose and escaped to the Federal lines, and were saved from the rebel conscription.

CHAPTER XLI.

VICKSBURG, MISS.

1. Now it came to pass, that after the great and mighty cities of New Orleans and Memphis, as well as all the province of Tennessee looking toward the West, and all the land of Mississippi lying toward the North, had fallen into the hands of the Federals:

2. Great fear fell upon the people of Vicksburg, lest their city should also be taken.

3. And they collected a great many negroes, and commenced building walls and digging ditches, and preparing themselves to fight against the Federal forces.

4. Vicksburg was a goodly city on the Eastern shore of the great river: it standeth on a bluff, and overlooketh the surrounding regions.

5. And there was much wealth, and also much intelligence at this place, for the people had good

schools, and they educated their children with great care.

6. But, as they owned many slaves, they had not been accustomed to labor with their own hands;

7. And they had been in the habit of commanding and not of being commanded;

8. Hence, they resolved to collect a great army, and fight for the possession of their city.

9. And they sent to Jefferson to aid them; and Jefferson sent them a great many troops, and a great many mighty guns, and huge engines of war, and powder and balls an infinite quantity

10. And the rebels made stupenduous works of defence, and called Vicksburg the "Gibraltar of America."

11. When Farragut, commonly called "Commodore," heard of these things, and how the rebels were making preparations for defence, his wrath was kindled against them.

12. And he said, who are these rebels that they should thus defy the forces of Uncle Sam?

13. And he swore in his wrath that he "would

smite them in battle, and lay waste their city," before the *ides* of March.

14. And he collected a great many gunboats, and took many men, and hastened to Vicksburg, swearing that he would level the disloyal city with the dust.

15. And the Confederates heard of his coming, and got ready to receive him.

16. And when he had come near to the city, he threw a bombshell at it to get the range, and the rebels threw shells at the ships;

17. And the bombardment progressed many days, but as the forces were far apart, little damage was done.

18. And the Confederates continued to strengthen their fortifications by day and by night;

19. And Jefferson sent them military men, regular "West-Pointers," to command them, and to advise them, and to assist them in making their fortifications, the wonder of all mankind.

20. And when the Federal commanders saw that the rebels would make resistance so formidable, they hesitated to attack them in their stronghold.

CHAPTER XLII.

SIEGE OF VICKSBURG.

1. Now it came to pass, that word was brought to Abraham, that Vicksburg was strongly fortified, and that the rebels had a large army ready to fight.

2. And the matter vexed Abraham, and when food was set before him he refused to eat, and the spirit of sleep departed from him.

3. And William, his Prime Minister, came into his presence, and gave him a pomegranate, and a little parched corn, and a glass of lemonade.

4. And when Abraham was a little revived, William said, "O Abraham, live forever!"

5. And Abraham said, "Say on, William, for thou art my most faithful friend, and my wisest counsellor."

6. And Abraham fell on William's neck and kissed him.

7. And William lifted up his voice, and said unto Abraham, "Our army and our boats can be made to pass this cruel and wicked city without shedding blood;

8. For, if your excellency seeth fit, a canal can be dug from the river above Vicksburg to the river below, because the river bendeth in the shape of a horse-shoe.

9. And the water from the great river, will flow into this canal, and boats can pass along, and not have to come under the guns of the rebel fort.

10. And, moreover, William said, if the water is once let into the canal, it will by its own action, deepen the channel, and widen it banks;

11. And, as the ancient "Father of Waters" is famous for odd whims, he will forsake his wonted channel, and run in that prepared by Federal soldiers.

12. Then will the wicked, rebel city stand miles away from the river, and become a deserted town;

13. And grass will grow in its streets, and the wild owl will hoot from its housetops, and the stork will make her nest in the palaces of the rich.

14. And the thing pleased Abraham, and he com-

manded a gold chain to be put upon Williams neck, and his photograph to be taken.

15. And Abraham sent messengers to Vicksburg, and commanded the Generals to set the men to work to dig the canal.

16. And the canal was dug.

17. But the water would not flow into it so as to be deep enough to float the mighty ships.

18. And Vicksburg still remained with its frowning fortifications and mighty guns.

CHAPTER XLIII.

BRAGG INVADES KENTUCKY.

1. About this time, Peter, whose surname is Beauregard, left the rebel army for a time.

2. And when Peter was gone, the command devolved upon Braxton, whose surname is Bragg.

3. Braxton was a brave man and a great warrior. He was with Gen. Taylor in Mexico, and won imperishable fame in the battles of that war.

4. And Braxton was in the battle of Shiloh, and all the world knew that he was as brave as Cæsar.

5. Now, as he was in the chief command, he desired to distinguish himself still more, and to reap brighter laurels than ever hitherto.

6. So he determined to march his men to Chattanooga, which is a city of no mean repute in East Tennessee, and on the Tennessee river.

7. Chattanooga is in the midst of mountains, and

two great railroads cross each other at this point, for which cause, it was a point of interest to any force holding the adjacent country.

8. And Braxton marched his army to Chattanooga, and for sometime, his head-quarters were there

9. But as the Federals were a great way off, there was no prospect of a battle.

10. And Braxton being a man of war, was not satisfied, and he marched his army still further to the North.

11. And seeing that Gen. Buell was in Middle Tennessee, and all the Confederates needed clothes, Braxton made up his mind to make a raid into Kentucky.

12. Now the people of Kentucky are very industrious, and they are exceeding skillful in manufacturing cotton and woollen fabrics;

13. And Braxton said to himself, if I can get ahead of General Buell, and march into the interior of Kentucky, I can supply my men with clothing and many other needful things.

14. And he made haste to march into Kentucky, and he carried consternation whithersoever he went.

15. And the people of Louisville were greatly alarmed, for they said, ours is a great city, and we have all kinds of provender for man and beast.

16. But, if the rebel army come hither, they will spoil our city, burn up our temples, plunder our stores, and do us much harm.

17. Now, there is a great city on the Ohio, above Louisville, called, in the Anglo-Saxon, Cincinnati, but surnamed the "Queen City."

18. And the "Queen City" is the greatest in all the West, it deals in furniture, dry goods, provisions, and swine's flesh;

19. The merchants of that city are princes, and all the people are rich, and their very eyes stick out with fatness.

20. And when the people of Cincinnati, heard that Braxton was laying Kentucky waste, they feared that he would march even against their city; for it is over against Kentucky.

21. Then they collected themselves together, and took arms, and made ready to give the rebels battle.

22. And there was no little commotion among the

people, and they ceased not day and night, to think and talk of these things.

23. Now, Gen. Buell marched forth with a mighty army, and prepared to give battle to Braxton;

24. And they met at Perryville, in the province of Kentucky, and they joined battle there;

25. And the battle raged with great fury, and men of the same race slew each other by hundreds;

26. And the blood of brothers was made to mingle, and the bosom of our common mother was baptized in the blood of her children;

27. Then was the land filled with the voice of mourning, lamentation, and woe; for mothers wept for their sons, and would not be comforted.

28. And the cry of fatherless orphans arose up to Him who sits enthroned in the distant Heavens, and whose tender mercies are over all his works.

30. The victory was warmly contested, nor was it decisive; but Braxton determined not to invade Kentucky further, and fell back into Tennessee, carrying with him many thousand yards of Kentucky jeans.

CHAPTER XLIV.

JOHN H. MORGAN.

1. It has been written in these Chronicles, that Kentucky would not secede with the Gulf States, nor would she afford aid to Abraham to subdue them.

2. Nevertheless, there were many of her sons that did not lie idle, but took part in this deadly strife of brothers.

3. Some could not consent that this old Union should be dissolved; they loved the flag under which their fathers fought, and which had waved over them from the years of their infancy.

4. These left Kentucky and joined themselves to Abraham's army, some in one place and some in another.

5. There were others that loved the South, for, they said, it was a goodly land, a genial clime, and its sons

were magnanimous and brave, and its daughters fair, and they would not lift up arms against her.

6. Of these not a few arose, and went down to "Dixie," and joined the rebel army.

7. And among those that joined the rebel army, was John, whose surname is Morgan.

8. John was a man who loved pleasure, and sought to obtain money by many devices.

9. And he had learned many games upon cards, and was exceeding cunning therein, whereby he won large sums of money.

10. And he was a man of unbounded wit, and loved to jest and make sport, and no man ever lived upon the whole earth, that could circumvent him.

11. And John sent unto Jefferson and said, "behold, I sympathize with thee and with the South, and I stand ready to serve thee."

12. And Jefferson sent him a letter of welcome and a commission; but as John was not a "West Pointer," Jefferson would not appoint him to a high office.

13. And John became the chief of a band of horsemen, and they went through Tennessee and Kentucky, and greatly vexed the people;

14. For they took their horses and their mules, and entered into their store-houses and took their goods, and scrupled not to accept their "greenbacks" when they could find them.

15. And they performed many deeds which made them a terror to the land, and exceedingly famous; but of these deeds shall they not be recorded in a future chapter?

CHAPTER XLV.

ESCAPE OF A REBEL CONSCRIPT.

1. Now it came to pass about this time, that there was great commotion in "Dixie" because of the Conscription.

2. For men said one to another, "How can we leave our homes, and wives, and little ones, and go to war?"

3. And they were slow to rally to the standard of King Jefferson, and he sent recruiting officers to take them by force, and make them fight against the Yankees.

4. Then did many Southern men flee from their homes, and live in caverns, and dens, and desert places of the earth; and not a few fled to Illinois, Indiana, and other places, where no rebel recruiting officer could come.

5. In the midst of these troublesome times there dwelt in "Dixie," in the province of Arkansas, a

certain man, whose name was Robert, surnamed Duvall.

6. And he was a just man, for he feared God, and loved his wife, attended church, and paid the preacher.

7. And Robert was in the prime of life, for he was not young nor was he old, and he was a strong man, and capable of performing much labor.

8. And when the Rebellion broke out, Robert was a Union man, and voted against Secession.

9. And it grieved him to think that the old flag, once so venerated and loved,—the flag which had ever commanded respect on every ocean and in every port, should be dishonored and made to trail in the dust.

10. And he argued with his neighbors, saying, What good is there in Secession, and how shall we be profited thereby?

11. Has not our country prospered ever since the Revolutionary war? Have not our possessions extended until we are a mighty nation, and feared by all men that dwell upon the face of the whole earth?

12. Have we not great and growing cities, that are rich in silver and gold, and lambs' wool, and bears' oil, and purple, and fine linen?

13. And are we not free, and vote for whom, we please, and no man has a right to say to any, *do this* or *do that?*

14. And do not our courts and our laws afford us ample protection?

15. Nay, ye cannot gainsay these things: then, why will ye lay aside this government for another? Why will ye depart from the faith of your fathers?

16. And his neighbors said unto him, O hard of heart, and slow to believe! Do ye not know that Abraham is elected President?

17. And he answered and said, *I know it.*

18. Then they said unto him, Abraham is an abolitionist, and intends to set our negroes free, and he is opposed to all Southern measures; and we will not have him to rule over us!

19. And Robert said, Abraham cannot set the negroes free, nor can he oppress the South; for, behold there is a majority against him in the great Sanhedrim, and he is sworn to support the Constitution, and to execute the laws of the land, and we need fear nothing he can do.

20. Then were they angry with Robert, and said,

thou art no friend to the South, but thou art a traitor and shall not continue so to speak among us.

21. Then was Robert afraid, for well did he know that his neighbors did not fear God, and that they were possessed of the Devil.

22. So Robert communed with his wife, and she advised him to set his house in order, and flee to the North.

23. And Robert did all that he could to get ready, for he needed some script for his journey, and he must needs provide for his family;

24. And when he was almost ready to leave them, a recruiting officer, with a file of men, came by night, and surrounded his house, and broke open his doors, and seized him;

25. And they took him to a rebel camp, and gave him a gun, and treated him as a soldier.

26. And it grieved Robert sorely, and he determined never to fight against the Union.

27. And his regiment marched to Tennessee, and they lay in camp at Columbus several months, and Robert was with them.

28. Now when Gen. Grant came against the rebel

army encamped on the great river named Mississippi, that regiment was in the battle, and Robert was in the thickest of the fight.

29. But he fired not a gun against the Federals, although he was in much danger from their guns.

30. And the Federals pressed sore against the Rebels, and they fled, and great confusion ensued;

31. And when they were greatly confused, Robert threw himself in the way of the approaching legions, and allowed himself to be taken as a prisoner;

32. Then was he taken to Cairo, and subsequently, on taking the oath of allegiance, he was released.

CHAPTER XLVI.

DUVALL GOES TO DIXIE FOR HIS FAMILY.

1. Now, when Robert was free from the rebel army, and no longer a prisoner of war, he began to consider how he should get his family away from Dixie.

2. And he devised many means, but none of them, on due reflection, seemed feasible.

3. For he feared both the Conscription and the violence of a lawless mob;

4. And he feared also, that his wife and babes would be left to starve.

5. And seeing no way to reach his family, he remained with Grant's army, but he was unhappy, because he mourned for his family lest he should see them no more.

6. In the meanwhile, Memphis fell, and the Federal army restored the old flag to its wonted place in that city, and Robert came to Memphis;

7. Now, was Robert much nearer his family, and began to devise means to go to them, and bring them away from Arkansas.

8. For he was afraid to venture beyond the Federal lines, lest the iron grasp of Conscription should again lay hold upon him.

9. And, behold, he purchased a wig full of gray hairs, and a pair of false whiskers for an old man, and disguised himself as an old man, too old to be conscripted:

10. Then he set forth from Memphis, and traveled on foot through the Mississippi bottom, to Crawley's Ridge, and proceeded thence to White river.

11. And those that saw him, said, This is an old man, and gray-headed, and they did not conscript him.

12. And he traveled many days, and over many hills, and across many streams that flow from the North, and swell the tide of the Arkansas, and he came to his house.

13. Then did he learn that the rebels had taken his horses, and his oxen, and all his valuables, and his family had procured bread with much difficulty.

14. And he passed among his old neighbors as a very old man, and an uncle of his wife, from Tennessee, for, in his disguise, they did not know him.

15. And they sold their beds, and chairs, and some of their clothing; and he purchased an old horse and a very little wagon, and the whole family set out to Memphis.

16. And after many days of traveling, and much fatigue, and privations, they came to Memphis poor, but free from rebel oppression.

CHAPTER XLVII.

HON. A. H. STEPHENS.

1. And it came to pass, after the South had seceded, that many of her noble sons loved the Union still.

2. Among these was Alexander, of the tribe of Georgia, who had been a member of the great Sanhedrim at Washington.

3. He was a man small in stature, but his nature was noble, and he was valiant, and eloquent of speech.

4. And he was a man of mighty influence. His fame had gone abroad into all the world, and all men delighted in his words, and believed him among the great men of the earth.

5. And Alexander opposed Secession. He wrote against it in the papers, and he made eloquent speeches against it in the halls of Congress, and his logic was powerful and could not be resisted.

6. But no eloquence could resist the overwhelming tide of Secession; nor could any logic deter the infuriated leaders.

7. Speech after speech fell from Alexander's eloquent lips. He invoked the gods to save the country from disruption! He conjured his countrymen by all the ties that bind man to man!

8. But all was in vain, for Secession was their Idol, and most devoutly did they worship at its shrine.

9. And Georgia voted herself out of the Union, and bade defiance to Federal sway.

10. Now, when Alexander saw that he had spoken in vain, and that his State had seceded, despite his efforts to the contrary,

11. His soul was sore vexed, and he lifted up his voice and wept, and said, "O, my country, my country! land of the Palmetto and the stately Magnolia!"

12. "Would that I had died for thee!" And he refused to be comforted.

13. And he said, "How can I leave thee, O my native land! Can I live when I see thee humbled in

the dust, thy altars desecrated, and all thy glory departed!"

14. And he sat in sackcloth and ashes for the space of forty days.

15. And all the world knew that Alexander, whose surname was Stephens, was a Union man, and hostile to Secession.

16. But it came to pass, when Georgia had really seceded, and the "Stars and Bars" had superseded the "Stars and Stripes."

17. That Alexander became less hostile to rebel rule, for he spake no more against it, but communed often with Jefferson and other leaders of the rebellion.

18. And when the people saw that he had ceased to oppose disunion, they said one to another, "Let us deal kindly with Alexander, and, peradventure, he may become one of our leaders."

19. And it came to pass, that the people voted, that Alexander should be a mighty chief among them, and sit on the right hand of King Jefferson.

20. And thereupon he became a Secessionist, and so continues unto this day.

CHAPTER XLVIII.

BRIGADIER JEFF.

1. And it came to pass in those days, when Claiborne, whose surname is Jackson, was Tetrarch over all Missouri, which being interpreted was Governor thereof,

2. That there was one "Jeff.," whose surname is Thompson, a man of repute among the Secessionists.

3. Now, "Jeff." was a man exceeding tall in stature, but he was spare made, and exceeding slender.

4. Before the war, he had been much in the regions about the "Lead Mines," and knew exactly the location of every grog-shop in all that land.

5. Now "Jeff." was a "blackleg," which (being interpreted) means a gambler.

6. And brandy and old Bourbon was sweeter to his taste than honey or the honey comb.

7. And it came to pass, that when these were not

at hand, "Jeff." scrupled not to imbibe large quantities of the vilest "tangle-foot."

8. And "Jeff." was a rebel, and he was brave, impulsive, and fond of adventure.

9. Now, when the rebellion broke out, and Missouri was hesitating whether to secede or not, "Jeff." gathered a band of desperadoes around him, and they carried desolation through all those parts.

10. And when Jefferson the Great, at Richmond, heard of these things, he sent unto him a commission as a Brigadier.

11. Then did many rebels flock to the standard of Brigadier "Jeff.," and they carried on a regular war against all Union men in South-Eastern Missouri.

12. And they performed many daring exploits in the regions round about New Madrid and Cape Giradeau.

13. And when the people heard of these things, they praised "Jeff," saying one to another, behold he is the "Marion" of this war.

14. And "Jeff." often came down to Memphis, for as yet, that city had not fallen into the hands of the Federals.

15. And when he was in the city, he always imbibed too freely, and was not unfrequently unable to navigate.

16. Now it came to pass, that when the Federals came to smite Memphis, "Jeff." was there.

17. And when the battle waxed warm, he rode a spotted pony, and scampered around upon the Bluff, and disharged his pistol at the approaching fleet.

18. And when they came near to the shore, it came to pass that "Jeff." wheeled to the "right about," and skedadd ed far away into the land of Dixie, and prepared to perform other deeds of noble daring.

CHAPTER XLIX.

PEGGY AND LITTLE JIMMY.

1. And it came to pass, when Tennessee had joined the Southern Confederacy, that her young men in thousands flocked to the rebel army.

2. And Jefferson sent them Generals, and arms, and ammunition, and bade them God-speed.

3. Now, there dwelt in a certain city, a man named James, but in the Anglo-Saxon, he was called Carson.

4. And James was a cultivator of the soil, and continually coaxed the earth to produce corn, flax, potatoes, cabbage, and other things of the like character.

5. And James was an industrious man, for no one ever saw him lying at the door of a grog-shop, or lounging in a saloon;

6. And he was an honest man, doing unto all men according to the golden rule.

7. And James read the newspapers, attended church, voted at elections, and served on juries.

8. And everybody called him "honest, red-headed, good-natured Jimmy."

9. And it came to pass, when Isham, whose surname is Harris, the Governor of Tennessee, had called for volunteers,

10. And all James' neighbors were volunteering, that James also joined a company, and made ready to go to the wars.

11. Now, James loved Peggy his wife, and *little Jimmy*, his son, and, when he thought of leaving them, his eyes grew red, and tears rolled down his cheeks.

12. And it came to pass that the company was organized, and the regiment was formed, and the officers commissioned, and all were mustered into service.

13. And the regiment was sent to Union City, a place of little repute, which standeth in West Tennessee, hard by the Obian country.

14. And in process of time, the regiment was removed to Columbus, and was in the great battle of Belmont.

15. And after many months, Columbus was evacuated, and the rebel army fell back by degrees, to Corinth, in North Mississippi.

16. And Braxton, whose surname is Bragg, was in command at Corinth, and all the men and Generals submitted to him.

17. And while the army was at Corinth, behold there came a messenger to James, saying, "Arise, and get thee home, for Peggy and little Jimmy are both lying sick of a fever, and nigh unto death."

18. And James arose and procured a furlough for ten days, and hastened home to see his wife and child.

19. And it came to pass that little Jimmy died. His little eyes became dim, and their light went out forever.

20. And they put linen white and clean upon the child, and laid him in a little coffin, and then it was placed in the cold and silent grave.

21. Now, when James had seen his little boy die and go down to the tomb, he mourned for him and refused to be comforted.

22. And Peggy was sick, and her strength was gone.

23. And James lifted up his voice and wept; and one came unto him, and said, "Why weepest thou?"

24. And James answered and said, "My soul is exceeding sorrowful; for my furlough expireth on the morrow, and Peggy will die, and I cannot remain with her to console her in her dying hour!"

25. Then said his friends, "But you must not go away until Peggy dies, and sleeps in peace along with little Jimmy; then mayst thou depart and be with the army."

26. But James answered and said, "Men will call me a deserter, and Braxton will condemn me to death!"

27. Then said his friends, "Are not the officers men? Have they not souls that can feel sympathy for another's woes. Tell them of thy case, and they will not blame thee!"

28. And James hearkened to his friends, and remained at the bedside of his dying wife.

29. And Peggy died, and James laid her in the grave, close to their little Jimmy.

30. And on the morrow he arose before day, and

hastened away to Corinth, having overstayed his furlough one day.

31. And when he was come to the army, he was seized and put under guard, and accused of desertion.

32. And a court-martial was called, and he was tried by them.

33. And James told them of Peggy and of Jimmy, and how they died, and he had buried them.

34. But they turned a deaf ear to all that he said, and condemned him to be shot for desertion.

35. Then his friends comforted him, saying, "Braxton is not a dog, that he should approve this sentence! Hath he not a wife and children?"

36. But behold! Braxton *did* approve the sentence, and the hour of execution was drawing nigh.

37. And in the night, when it was dark, and the guards slept, James arose, and laid aside the cords that bound him and fled!

38. And the guards awaked and fired their guns at him, and wounded him on the face.

39. But James made his escape and fled from Corinth, and he came unto Pittsburg, upon the Tennessee river, and joined himself unto the Federals.

40. And Abraham sent him a captain's commission, and he remained with the Federal army, and fought against Braxton.

41. And James is in the Federal army unto this day.

CHAPTER L.

CLINTON, WHOSE SURNAME WAS CHASE.

1. Now when James, whose surname is Buchanan, was yet Chief Ruler, and in the last year of his reign,

2. It came to pass that there was a certain young man in the "Buckeye" State, whose name was Clinton, but his surname was Chase.

3. And Clinton was a young man, and he was of an honorable family, handsome and comely to look upon.

4. Moreover he was a good scholar, for he had studied many books in the Wesleyan University, which standeth in a place called Delaware, in the province of Ohio.

5. And Clinton had heard from the South, that teachers were highly honored, and that the Southern people gave them much money.

6. So Clinton arose and put on his sandals, and a

leathern girdle, and took his journey to the Southern country.

7. And when he had traveled many days, he came to a part of the country, known as Eudora, in the province of Arkansas.

8. And Clinton taught the youth of Eudora, and caused them to increase in knowledge, until his fame went abroad into all the regions round about.

9. And it came to pass that the people of Lake Village, which standeth not a great way off from Eudora, heard of the fame of Clinton.

10. Then said they one to another, "Let us send for Clinton, that he may come to our town, even unto Lake Village, and instruct our children, lest they live fools and die dunces."

11. And they sent letters to Clinton, and invited him to come; and they promised him a large sum of gold, if he would teach their children.

12. And Clinton arose and went to Lake Village. And the people made him a good school, and he lived with them, and taught their children.

13. And the children loved Clinton, for he was kind

unto them, and dealt with them as though he was an elder brother.

14. And the parents loved him, because he was faithful to teach their children, and fully earned all the gold they gave him.

15. And the young maidens loved Clinton, because he was young and handsome, and had an intellectual face and bright, black eyes, and each one hoped that she might stir up the tender passion in his bosom.

16. And the preachers loved Clinton, because he was moral, and attended church, and listened to them with much attention and respect.

17. And Clinton lived at Lake Village, until the war cry arose, and swept over the land of the South.

18. And when Abraham had been chosen Chief Ruler, and South Carolina had seceded,

19. Arkansas also, seceded, and the people were wroth with Abraham, and began to make war against him and the North.

20. But Clinton still taught the youth of Lake Village, and they did mightily increase in knowledge.

21. But when the young men of Lake Village were

preparing to go forth to battle, they asked him to go with them, but he said nay.

22. But the time was at hand when brother should go forth against brother, and son against father, and father against son, and the spirits of men waxed warm.

CHAPTER LI.

LAKE PROVIDENCE.

1 Now Clinton's soul clove to the Union, but he abhored the sound of disunion.

2. Moreover he loved his school, and did not wish to leave it.

3. And he said nought to give offence to any man, for he knew that the people would not suffer a lover of the Union to abide with them.

4. Now it came to pass, that when the people heard of the great battle of Manassas, they rejoiced exceedingly, because the Confederates had prevailed against the Yankees.

5. Then the people told Clinton, that the war would soon end—that Washington would fall before Peter, whose surname is Beauregard, and that many of the Free States would come over to the South.

6. And it came to pass, that many who had been

Union men, now hated the Union and loved King Jefferson, and went forth with him to battle.

7. But it soon came to pass that the Federals pressed the Rebels sore; Bowling Green, a walled city, Forts Henry and Donelson, mighty fortresses, and Nashville, also a walled city, fell, and the rebel army went back in haste to the provinces of Alabama and Mississippi.

8. Then did Jefferson send out a proclamation into all the South, commanding the Governors of the States to enrol and send forth a vast army.

9. And it came to pass, that the Federals smote Columbus, and overcame it, and New Madrid and Island No. 10.

10. Then went there a mighty rumor through all the land, that the Yankees were coming to Memphis, and great fear fell upon the people.

11. And the people of Arkansas, were sore vexed, and they said one to another, "Let others do as they may, but as for us, we will die rather than have the Yankees rule over us."

12. Then did Jefferson send forth a commandment,

for all that loved the South to gird on their sword and prepare to smite the Yankees.

13. And Clinton was afraid to abide longer in Lake Village, lest he should be forced to fight for King Jeff.

14. So he departed from that country, and went into Lake Providence, in the province of Louisiana.

15. And when he was come to Lake Providence, he showed letters that the people of Lake Village had given him;

16. And the letters spake well of him and said, that he was an excellent teacher of youth, and a good citizen.

17. And when the people read the letters and saw that he had a goodly face, they said "he is a good man and true, and they took him to their houses and put meat before him;

18. And they gave him water to wash his feet, and some parched corn, and bade him welcome to their town.

19. And they made up a school for him, and he taught their children, and mingled not in public affairs.

20. But soon the people of Lake Providence also began to make ready to go forth against the Yankees.

21. And they besought Clinton to join himself unto them, and to go forth with them to battle.

22. But Clinton said, "Nay; I pray thee have me excused," and this vexed the people, and they uttered threats against him.

23. And when they were ready to go forth, they went up the mighty river to Memphis, and thence to Corinth.

CHAPTER LII.

STARTLING INTELLIGENCE.

1. Now this company had not been many days at Corinth, when word came to Lake Providence,

2. Behold Beauregard hath evacuated Corinth, and gone further toward the South.

3. Then were the people sore distressed; for, they said, "these Yankee invaders are taking from us all our country."

4. But the papers said that Beauregard was a great General, and acted with great wisdom in retreating with his hosts.

5. Notwithstanding, the people did not believe it, and feared that the Southern Confederacy would soon be no more.

6. About this time a messenger came down the river, and said that Fort Pillow must surely fall;

7. Because a mighty army had surrounded it, and a fleet of mighty ships with iron armor were on the river, and were even then pouring upon the rebel fort, a storm of cannon balls and bombshells;

8. Then the people laid aside their work, and thought of nothing else, but of Fort Pillow and the the approach of the dreaded foe.

9. And for the space of seven days, there was no news from that direction, for few boats were now running on the great river.

10. And the people greatly wondered what had become of the gunboats, for more than two score of them had gone up the river

11. And one answered and said "Never mind our gunboats,—they will take care of themselves, and of Memphis, too!"

12. Now it came to pass, on a certain day about this time, at the third hour of the evening, of the selfsame day,

13. That a smoke was descried in the distance, up the river, and soon the chimneys of two steamers were discernable;

14. Then did the population, men, women, children

and negroes, assemble at the wharf-boat impatient to hear the news.

15. And when the boats drew near, by the aid of the telescope, their names were read, and they were found to be the transport *Paul Jones* and the gunboat *Earl Van Dorn!*

16. And they were making great haste.

17. And a certain planter lifted up his voice and said, What aileth the *Van Dorn?*

18. For her sides are pierced in many places, and her ensign is hanging in shreds, and her wheel-house is bored through and through!

19. And the multitude cried out, "What's the news?"

20. And the captain of the *Paul Jones*, lift up his voice, and said, "Memphis is fallen—is fallen! The Bluff City is this day, in the hands of the blue coats!"

21. Then did the people curse and swear, and ceased not day and night to damn the Abolitionists, and Abe Lincoln, and all that dwell beyond the line, surnamed Mason and Dixon's.

22. And they mourned for Memphis, and said,

"Alas! that great city! that mighty city! that city of cotton and molasses."

23. And they smote upon their breasts and refused to be comforted.

24. And the people asked many questions of the men on the gunboats, and the men said,

25. "All our gunboats are lost, but the *Van Dorn* and we alone are left to tell thee."

26. Moreover, they said that the Federal gunboats had chased them, and were even then not far behind!

27. So saying, the *Van Dorn* departed in haste for the sluggish waters of the Yazoo.

CHAPTER LIII.

SENSATION.

1. Now it came to pass when the boats were out of sight, that a prominent Secesh planter stood upon a hogshead of molasses, and cried out,

2. "Men and brethren, what shall we do?"

3. And when the people saw that he spake in real Secesh style, they gave him the greater heed.

4. And he said, The Southern Confederacy is a "goner," and no mistake;

5. For now these blue coats have taken Memphis, and their gunboats are on this river, and some of them will be here before the setting of the sun.

6. And they will batter down our town, and burn our houses, confiscate our negroes, and carry away all our goods!

7. And great fear fell upon all present, and they

ran to their houses, and fell to work, packing up their goods, and money, and silver plate.

8. And many of them fled into the country.

9. But behold the sun went down and rose again many times, and the gunboats came not;

10. And the people said, peradventure, they will not come at all; but as they began thus to speak, behold they were even then in sight.

11. And they came along down the river, and did not so much as whistle a salute to the little town, where Clinton lived

12. And behold they were going to Vicksburg, a rumor had gone forth that the rebels had built great walls about that city, and were determined to defend it to the last.

13. And when the Federal gunboats came near to the city, they threw great shells at it; but the rebels were too many in number for the Federal force;

14. So the gunboats returned, and left Vicksburg, and the people rejoiced, saying, "Vicksburg cannot be taken!"

CHAPTER LIV.

THE ESCAPE.

1. Now it came to pass that Clinton greatly desired to depart from the Southern country and go again to live among his own kin, even the dwellers of the North.

2. But King Jefferson had many spies in that region called *Vigilance Committees*, and it became necessary for Clinton to keep a watch over his mouth and a guard upon his tongue.

3. He determined, that if he must fight, he would fight *for*, but not *against* the Union.

4. And as there could be no more schools in that region, Clinton was lonely and sad, and sighed to escape from the tyranny to which he was subjected.

5. And when the gunboats passed by, he stood upon the shore and made signals for them to stop, but not knowing him or his designs, they would not stop.

6. And he sought to obtain a small ship commonly called a skiff, and to make his escape to Memphis, so that he might come within the Federal lines.

7. But the skiffs were all taken away or destroyed, and he could not effect his purpose.

8. And it came to pass that, while he was yet teaching the youth of Lake Providence, a recruiting officer came along, and conscripted Clinton;

9. But Jefferson had commanded that any teacher, who had a score of scholars or more, should not be required to go forth to battle contrary to his will.

10. And Clinton was released from conscription, because he had more than a score of scholars.

11. And one came privately unto him, and said, "O Clinton, make haste and get thee away from Lake Providence!

12. "For thou art a Northern man, and as thou hast not gone into the army, the people suspect that thou art a Union man;

13. "And thou art no longer safe in '*these diggings!*' Therefore, I beseech thee, arise and flee."

14. Then was Clinton greatly afraid, lest the Secesh

should press him into the army, or cast him into prison to die of neglect.

15. And now when Clinton no longer taught the youth, behold he was conscripted again;

16. And seeing that he could no more plead exemption, he resolved to make his escape to the Federal lines.

17. And Clinton arose and left Lake Providence, and went into a desert place, hard by the brink of the great river, that he might get upon a Federal ship, if any, should pass that way.

18. But the eyes of the spies were upon him, and he could not make his escape.

19. And Clinton fled to the woods, because the time was close at hand, when he must go to the rebel army;

20. And he stood upon the river, and called to all the Federal boats he saw passing, and made signs for them to stop, but they would not.

21. And he was three days and nights among wolves, and panthers, and other wild beasts, for he feared the rabid Secesh more than they.

22. And Clinton's heart sank within him, when he

saw that the boats would not heed his signals, and that in a few days he must be in the rebel army.

23. Then he arose and returned to Lake Providence, and behold there were many Rebel soldiers there.

24. Now, it was told to Clinton, "behold a certain man is here, who is going to Vicksburg in a buggy."

25. And Clinton approached the man, and said, "May I go with thee to Vicksburg?"

26. And fearing to journey alone, the man was glad to have Clinton to go with him.

27. And Clinton went with him in his buggy, and the guards let them pass;

28. And Clinton left all his goods at Lake Providence, and went to Vicksburg, and when they arrived near the city,

29. He turned aside to the Federal fleet, that was exchanging prisoners, and the man rode in the buggy to Vicksburg.

30. And Clinton made his escape, and lives at the North to this day.

CHAPTER LV.

SOUTHERN DIVINES.

1. And it came to pass in those days of Secession and civil discord, that few persons in all the South, failed to mingle in the noisy strife.

2. Judges, who sat upon the bench, and in whose hands property, reputation, and even life itself, were often placed, became noisy politicians, and urged the people to destroy the government whose Constitution they had sworn to support.

3. And reverened divines, whose mission was one of peace, and whose treasure ought to have been laid up in heaven, laid aside their holy calling.

4. And, instead of pointing penitents to a throne of Divine Grace, they preached Secession, and urged men to quit not their sins, but the Union.

5. They ceased to preach Christ and Him crucified, and failed not to preach Secession, Jeff. Davis, and the South.

6. And not a few of these sons of Levi were so much incensed against Abraham and the Abolitionists of the North, that they laid aside their sacred calling.

7. And they came down from their pulpits, shut up their churches, abandoned their spiritual flocks, gathered up their guns, and marched away to fight for Secession and the South.

8. And some of them became captains, and some majors, and some colonels, and one of them, who in times of peace was a Bishop, became a Major-General in the rebel army.

9. Then did the cause of Zion languish, iniquity in high places abounded, and the love of many waxed cold.

10. And hundreds of churches remained closed; the voice of devotion arose not from their altars, and the owls sat on their eaves, and hooted up to the rising moon.

11. Preachers left their circuits, and learned the use of carnal weapons, and often engaged in mortal strife.

12. And it came to pass that those who remained at home and continued to preach to their people,

observed all the fasts and thanksgiving days appointed by Jeff. Davis.

13. Now, when the Federals took Nashville, and New Orleans, and Memphis, the preachers who were in these cities, were fearful to pray for the Southern Confederacy.

14. But they would not pray for "Uncle Abraham," or the Government of the United States.

15. And when the President proclaimed a day of Thanksgiving, and all the friends of the Union came together to praise the Lord for success in battle, these Southern divines came not.

16. And although Holy Writ commands to pray for "Kings, and all that are in authority," and even for our enemies," still, no Southern minister lifted up his voice in prayer for any one in authority in the North.

17. Nor would they have anything to do with Federal chaplains, even of the same order, nor regard them as members of the Christian Church.

18. And a spirit of bitterness sprang up between them, and between churches of the same faith and they spake evil one of another, and sinned before the Lord.

19. Oh! that men would cease to practice the rude arts of war! and learn to live in peace!

20. Then would the earth blossom as the rose, and the solitary places would be made glad.

CHAPTER LVI.

LEE MARCHES INTO MARYLAND.

1. Now George was commanded by Abraham to take charge of the armies encamped round about Washington, and to defend that city.

2. And General Pope tarried in the land of Virginia.

3. Now the chiefs of the army of Dixie were wily and full of cunning, and it came to pass that they brought thirty legions secretly between the hosts of the North and the Capital City.

4. Now when this was known, Pope called unto his chief captains,

5. Unto McDowell, and Sigel, and Kearney, and Reno, and Hooker, and Porter,

6. And commanded that they should go forth with many legions and overtake squadrons of the Rebels, and put them to the sword and scatter them.

7. Now the armies met even on the same field on which the battle of Bull Run had happened.

8. And terrible was the noise of the conflict, and great was the carnage, and many gave up the ghost in the midst of the battle.

9. And the hosts of the Rebels prevailed mightily even so that the armies of Freedom fled and came over the river Potomac.

10. Now it came to pass not long after this thing, that the armies of the Rebels crossed over the river also, saying, surely will we go up against the cities of the Yankees,

11. Even against Harrisburg, and against Philadelphia, and against Washington, which is the stronghold of Lincoln.

12. And we will lay waste the lands of the tribes of the Yankees, and burn their houses with fire, and carry away their young men captive.

13. And we will seize upon Horace and Wendell the Abolitionist, and upon Henry Ward, and upon all those who have spoken hardly of us.

14. And all these will we hang to a tree even as

Haman was hanged, but Abraham will we hang to many trees.

15. Now went forth George from before the fortress of the Capitol, and led with him a great multitude of soldiers.

16. And with him went Hooker and Burnside, and many valiant captains for officers and leaders of legions.

17. And George set the battle in array against the proud foes of the nation, and came upon them like a great whirlwind.

18. And drove them before him with might and with power, and put them to the sword and smote them sore.

19. And thrashed them soundly, and beat them and licked them and made them skedaddle.

20. In two great contests did he flog them soundly, even in the battle of South Mountain and the fight of Antietam.

21. So they departed away out of the country and came unto the land of their fathers, and they spoiled not the land of the Yankees,

22. Nor seized upon Abraham nor upon Horace or Wendell.

23. After these things, Abraham visited the army, and reviewed it, and spake comforting words unto the people.

24. Nevertheless Abraham was grieved because George had not taken the Rebels captive, and prevented them from escaping out of our borders.

25. And Abraham was sore troubled because the wars were not ended, and he devised many ways by which he might hasten the day of peace, and bring joy to the people,

26. And pondered much on the sayings of Horace which had been written in a letter.

27. For Horace wrote unto Abraham, saying, of a truth thou wilt not prevail against the South until thou abolishest slavery,

28. For the Lord of Hosts will not help thee if thou helpest not his people who are in bondage, even his children the Ethiopians who are bound.

CHAPTER LVII.

ABRAHAM'S WARNING.

1. Now when Abraham had thought of all that Horace had written and counselled with himself, he called William, his chief counseller, and said unto him,

2. Is not Horace right in this thing? and are not the Ethiopians a great help unto Jefferson and a great harm unto us.

3. Are they not hewers of wood and drawers of water for him, and doth he not employ them to build his walls and dig his trenches, and to till his fields and to tend his flocks?

4. Verily, William, I will not that this be so, but as my soul liveth, I will deliver this people from bondage, and hire them with money that they come up and help us.

5. And the thing pleased William, and he told it

unto Salmon and unto many of the High Priests of the Sanhedrim, and they were glad.

6. So Abraham wrote a Proclamation, and caused the Great Seal of the Union to be set thereunto.

7. And Abraham's Proclamation was to the Rulers of the land of Dixie, and to all the slave-holders thereof.

8. And in the Proclamation it was written, "that on the first day of the first month of the year eighteen hundred and sixty and three, all persons held in bondage in any State or part of a State,

9. "The people whereof should be in rebellion against the United States should be thenceforward and forever free.

10. Now Abraham's Proclamation went forth through the length and breadth of the land.

11. And many were glad and rejoiced greatly, but some murmured, saying, Abraham hath no right to do this thing.

12. Others wondered, saying, how can this thing come to pass, and how shall the Ethiopians be free? Is Abraham a god that his word breaketh the bonds of the slave?

13. Others said, let be, we shall see how this thing will end; verily Abraham hath sense and knoweth his own way.

14. Now many of the captains and leaders of the armies resigned their offices, and would not serve in the wars after Abraham had done this thing.

15. And the chroniclers of the South wrote hard things of Abraham, calling him fiend, for they said he inciteth the servant to rise in rebellion against his master.

16. Nevertheless Abraham putteth his hands in his pockets, and walketh up and down and whistleth, for he knew his own way, and followed it.

CHAPTER LVIII.

BATTLE AT CORINTH.

1. Now about the beginning of the tenth month, while the army of Ulysses was encamped round about Corinth, came eight and thirty thousand Rebels against them.

2. And the Rebels were led by many mighty captains of the South, even by Van Dorn and Price and Lovell and Villepigue and Rust.

3. Then Ulysses spake unto a mighty chief called Rosecrans, and commanded that he should lead forth his men and set the battle in array against the Rebels.

4. And Rosecrans went forth and took with him four divisions.

5. The division of Hamilton, and the division of McKean and the division of Davies and the division of Stanley.

6. Now the forces of Rosecrans joined battle with the Rebels, and there was great slaughter.

7. And the Rebels fled, leaving their dead and their wounded, and their banners and three great guns and three thousand stand of arms.

8. And the number of Rebels that were slain was one thousand and four hundred and twenty and three.

9. And the number of Rebel prisoners taken was two thousand, two hundred and three score and five.

10. But the number of Federals that were slain was but three hundred, and of Federal prisoners there were but two hundred taken.

CHAPTER LIX.

PERRYVILLE.

1. Now it came to pass that Bragg, who was a mighty chief among the Rebels, came into the land of Kentucky, even nigh unto the city of Louisville, which is upon the river Ohio.

2. And the people of Louisville were full of fear, and cried out for help, saying, wherefore hath not Buell protected us.

3. Now Buell was a chief in the army of Abraham, and commanded one hundred thousand souls.

4. Therefore a cry went up from the city, that he should save the place from desolation, and from the sword of the Rebel.

5. But Buell and Bragg were brethren and would not willingly join their armies in battle.

6. And furthermore many said, surely Buell loveth the land of Dixie and the people thereof, and therefore will he not go against this host.

7. Nevertheless, Buell went against the Rebels, for he said, if I do not this thing, even my own soldiers will hate me, and peradventure Abraham also will deal hardly with me.

8. So on the tenth month, about the eighth day, Buell came upon the hosts of the Rebels, and joined battle with them.

9. And it was about the tenth hour when the battle began, and it continued until the evening.

10. But when darkness fell upon the armies, behold the Rebels fled into the land of Tennessee.

11. Then Buell gathered together his army and followed the troops of Bragg afar off, for he took no pleasure in fighting his brother.

12. Now the name of the battle that was fought by the hosts of Bragg and the hosts of Buell, was the battle of Perryville.

13. After these things, Abraham commanded that Buell should no longer be a leader in the armies of the nation, but he made Rosecrans to be commander in his place.

14. For Rosecrans was valiant, and of great wisdom, and much loved in the land.

15. And he had won great fame, because he had overcome the Rebels in the land of Mississippi, even at the battle of Corinth.

16. Now the people were glad when they knew that Rosecrans was made commander in the place of Buell.

CHAPTER LX.

CANE HILL AND PRAIRIE GROVE.

1. It came to pass in the twelfth month, and on the twentieth day that a great battle was fought in the land of Arkansas.

2. For in those days there was no peace to him that went out, nor to him that came in, but vexations, and wars were upon the inhabitants of all the countries.

3. Words came unto James, whose surname is Blunt, warning him that Marmaduke, with many Rebels, would fall upon the armies of the North and slay them.

4. But behold James was wary and valiant, and he fell upon Marmaduke and upon those that were with him, and put them to flight and killed many.

5. And the place on which they fought is called Cane Hill unto this day.

6. Afterwards came a great multitude of Rebels to

take vengeance upon James and upon his soldiers, because they had overcome Marmaduke.

7. And the great multitude was led by one whose name is called Hindman, who was a famous captain in the South.

8. But James sought aid of a brave chief, even of J. F., whose surname is Herron, who aforetime had fought valiantly.

9. And Herron joined his army unto the army of James, and they set the battle in array against the armies of the tribes of Dixie.

10. And fell upon them and smote them sorely, and put them to flight after a mighty conflict.

CHAPTER LXI.

BOMBARDMENT OF FREDERICKSBURG.

1. Now Abraham counselled with himself as to George, who is called Little Mac, who had long ruled over the army of the Potomac.

2. And Abraham saith, lo, this many months hath my servant George ruled the army of the Potomac, and hath not prevailed over the enemies of the people,

3. Therefore will I remove him out of his place, and Burnside shall rule in his stead.

4. Now all this was done even as the heart of Abraham desired, and Burnside became ruler in the stead of George.

5. Furthermore, Burnside re-organized the army, and established many new rules therein, and put all things in readiness that he might go against the enemy.

6. And Abraham commanded that the soldiers should observe and keep the Sabbath day, for Abra-

ham was a holy man, and desired the Scriptures to be fulfilled.

7. After all things were in readiness, Burnside led forth his hosts unto the banks of the river Rappahannock, which floweth nigh unto the city of Fredericksburg.

8. And he caused two bridges to be made over the river and crossed over, both he and those that were with him, and he set the battle in array against the city.

9. For the Rebels had gathered themselves together at Fredericksburg, and built walls about them, and had digged trenches that the Federals might not pass over.

10. But Burnside had mighty engines of war, even great guns of iron and of brass,

11. Which sent forth balls of iron, and shell, and destructive missiles to spoil the works of the Rebels.

12. And the battle was furious, and many were killed on both sides, and many were sore wounded, and some fled, but Burnside could not destroy the city nor cause the Rebels to fly.

13. So after three days had passed, and the even-

ing of the fourteenth of the twelfth month had come, the army of the Potomac withdrew, and crossed again over the river Rappahannock, and returned even by the way they had come.

14. Now when Abraham heard how valiantly the soldiers had fought, and how they had obeyed their Chief in all things, he wrote a letter unto the soldiers,

15. Thanking them for their great labor, and mourning with them in their failure, and saying many words of encouragement.

16. But the people murmured because Burnside had not put every soul of the Rebels to the edge of the sword.

CHAPTER LXII.

SHERMAN'S ATTACK ON VICKSBURG.

1. AFTER these things, William, whose surname is Sherman, went forth against Vicksburg,

2. With one hundred transports on which were troops, and arms, and horses and munitions of war.

3. Now this mighty fleet went out from Memphis, with music and rejoicing, with the beating of drums and the streaming of banners.

4. And sailed down the Father of Waters, even the river Mississippi, unto the river Yazoo which floweth through the land of Mississippi, and near unto Vicksburg.

5. And on a certain day they landed and went up against the Rebels, who were encamped about the city.

6. But behold when a week had well nigh passed, and they had not been able to reach the city, because of its strong defences and because of the valor of its defenders.

7. William called together his followers, and commanded that they should enter into the boats and depart from the valley of the Yazoo.

8. So they entered into the boats as William had commanded, and withdrew themselves from attacking the Rebels.

9. And newspaper reporters derided William in their letters, saying, behold he hath attempted much and accomplished nothing.

10. Verily, hath this expedition proven a fizzle, and the transports of William have basely skedaddled.

11. Now the news correspondents were wise men and prophets, and spake many things for the edification of all men.

12. Howbeit many of them wrote much of themselves and magnified their own names exceedingly, so that the heaven of heavens could not contain them.

CHAPTER LXIII.

STONE RIVER.

1. Now great was the rejoicing of the people when Rosecrans went out against the bands of the Rebels in the land of Tennessee.

2. For his heart fainted not, neither did he fear when he came nigh unto the battle, nor did he tremble in the presence of his enemies.

3. But he was gallant and brave, and led his armies forth to the battle with shouts and with gladness.

4. Seven days was heard the clangor of battle on the Stone River, round about the town of Murfreesboro.

5. And the arms of the Union triumphed gloriously, for the Lord of Hosts was with them, and His glory perched upon their banners,

6. And the minions of Davis were dismayed, and fled from the swords of the loyal, for brave were the captains that led forth the hosts of the Union.

7. And great was the skill and the valor of Rosey and strong were the arms of the soldiers.

8. And they smote the Rebels with the edge of the sword, and took many captive.

9. Howbeit many were slain of the tribes of the North-West, and the voice of lamentation was heard for the brave who had fallen.

10. "How are the mighty fallen in the midst of the battle. How are the mighty fallen, and the weapons of war perished."

11. Woe, woe unto the land of slavery, even unto the land of Traitors, because of the mourning that falleth upon the people.

12. Woe, woe unto those who have drawn the sword against the bosom of Freedom, for the day of their destruction cometh.

13. For the wrath of the Lord is kindled against them, and in His fierce anger they shall be con- consumed.

14. Famine and pestilence shall compass their cities, and the hand of violence shall crush their strong places.

CHAPTER LXIV.

PARSON BROWNLOW.

1. Now it has been written in these "Chronicles," that Southern preachers went after Secession, and no longer loved the Government of their fathers.

2. But there was one who would not have Jeff. Davis to rule over him, and his name was William and his surname was Brownlow.

3. Now, William was a mighty man in word and in deed—he had flocks, and herds, and cattle and man-servants and maid-servants; and, moreover, he was editor of a newspaper called the "Knoxville Whig."

4. And William was a prophet among the Methodists, and he prophecied in the regions of the Holstein, and French Broad, and other parts of the province of East Tennessee.

5. And when Tennessee seceded, William lifted up

his voice against the measure, and would not acknowledge the South as a rightful power.

6. Then were the people vexed with William, and they sent men to reason with him, to convince him, and to bring him over to Southern loyalty.

7. But William was angry, and would not hear them, but remained firm for the Union.

8. And he published many things in his paper against Jefferson and other leaders of the Rebellion; for William was brave, and feared not what man could do unto him.

9. And it came to pass when Jefferson heard of the sayings and doings of William, his wrath was kindled against him;

10. And he commanded the soldiers to take him and to cast him into prison, and he was put into the Knoxville jail.

11. And they fed William on bread and water, and threatened to put him to death, but William feared them not.

12. And they spoiled his house, and carried away his goods, and confiscated his lands.

13. But William was a man of mighty influence in the South; for many thousands knew him;

14. And they heard him prophecy, and he had nursed their children, and had slept on their beds, and broken bread at their tables:

15. And they had sung songs together at the same camp-meetings, and smoked from the same cob-pipes; and the souls of many clave unto William.

16. Now Jefferson feared that if he put William to death, the people would revolt, and cry out against him.

17. Therefore he commanded that William should be taken from jail in Knoxville, and conveyed Northward, even into the dominions of Abraham.

18. Then the soldiers took William from Knoxville, and they led him to Nashville, and he entered the Federal lines.

19. And the Federals heard that he was coming, and they went forth to meet him; and they put him in a chariot, and brought him into the city.

20. And they gave him some water to wash his feet, and they anointed his head with oil, and put meat before him, and a flagon of wine!

21. And when William saw these things, he bowed himself to the earth, and worshipped, saying,

22. Blessed be the Lord God of our fathers, who did raise up Washington and sustain him in the midst of the Revolutionary war;

23. And who did permit our fathers to build up this glorious Union, and make it the wonder of all nations!

24. And Thou, O Lord, hast preserved me amid many dangers, and led me from the hands of the rebels.

25. Preserve, O Lord, the Union; let not the vile rebels prevail against it; but keep it to the end of all time, as an asylum for the oppressed of all nations!

26. But curse Thou, Jeff. Davis, Bill Yancey, Kirby Smith, and every rebel, and hasten thou to break the back-bone of the Rebellion! Amen!

CHAPTER LXV.

PARSON BROWLOW.—(CONTINUED.)

1. AND when William had made an end of worshipping, he raised himself up, and sat at the table and did eat.

2. And after many days, William got upon a steamboat, and descended the Cumberland river, and went to Cincinnati.

3. Now Cincinnati is a mighty city, and it is called the "Queen City," for it hath a mighty trade in pork, hogs' lard, sausages, and spiced pigs' feet.

4. And when the people of Cincinnati heard of William's approach, they rejoiced greatly;

5. And they slew an ox, and seven turkeys, and a ewe-lamb,

6. And they made a great feast and bade William welcome!

7. And many thousands came to see William, and they brought gifts of silver and gold, and wine, and lambs' wool, and fine linen!

8. And William stood up before them and made a great oration.

9. And William told them how he loved the Union and opposed Secession,—and how he had suffered for opinion's sake, and why he was now come unto them.

10. And he spake for the space of one hour, and the Buckeyes hearkened to him, and treasured up all his sayings in their hearts!

11. And when he had made an end of speaking, they smote upon the palms of their hands, and jobbed with the end of their canes, and stamped with the heels of their boots;

12. And for the space of one hour and three quarters, they ceased not to cry out, "great have been the persecutions of William!"

13. And William abode with them many days.

14. Now, the land of the Hoosiers lieth to the West of that city, and it hath a great city named Indianapolis.

15. And William arose and went unto Indianapolis,

and the people flocked to hear him, for they had heard of his fame.

16. And he made a speech unto them, and they were greatly amused.

17. And William went to many other cities, and made orations, and ate dinners, and drank toasts, and offered up prayers.

18. And William's fame went into all the land.

19. And William wrote a book, and published it, and there were many pictures in it, and divers things to interest the people.

20. And William still loved the Union, and he sent to Knoxville, and brought away his wife and little ones.

21. And they crossed the river safe into Kentucky, and made their home in Covington, where they live unto this day

CHAPTER LXVI.

THE OLD MILLER IN NASHVILLE.

1. Now in these days it came to pass, that John, whose surname is Morgan, with about twelve hundred men, was in the province of Middle Tennessee.

2. And they burnt bridges, stopped trains, stole horses, robbed houses, and the hearts of the people sank within them.

3. And they were in many skirmishes in regions about Lebanon and Murfreesboro.

4. And they took many Federal prisoners, and sent them to Richmond to see what Jefferson would do with them.

5. And John was the most cunning of all men, insomuch that no man upon the face of the earth was like unto him.

6. When he saw that Nashville was full of Federals,

and that there were pickets on all sides, he laid aside his regimentals and his sword;

7. And he attired himself in the coarse garb of a miller, with a patched coat, and a slouched hat, and unsightly brogans;

8. And he drove a wagon with six oxen into the city, and the wagon was loaded with meal, and hens' eggs, and fresh butter.

9. And he passed the pickets; for they did not know that the miller was John Morgan, the rebel.

10. And he went into the city, and visited the market, and all the places of the city, and sold produce to all that would buy.

11. And John saw how many armed men was guarding the city, and how their fortifications were built.

12. Moreover, he sat at the table with the officers, and ate fried eggs with them, and drank brandy, and cracked jokes.

13. And they even spake together of John, and his late deeds, nor did they for a moment suppose that the old miller before them was the veritable John.

14. And John learned all that he cared to know, and

then he arose and took his ox-whip, and drove his wagon, and departed from the city.

15. And when the Federals found out that the old miller was no other than John, whose surname is Morgan, they feared greatly;

16. And they doubled their guards, and commanded every miller and egg-peddler to be arrested.

17. And John put on his uniform, and again took charge of his men, and set off on an expedition.

18. And all men feared John, because of his cunning, and the many deeds he performed.

CHAPTER LXVII.

THE EDICT OF EMANCIPATION.

1. Now when the year of Jubilee was come, Abraham numbered the tribes that were in rebellion and arms against the Union,

2. In the land of Texas, and the land of Arkansas, and the land of Louisiana, and the land of Mississippi, and the land of Alabama,

3. Of the land of Florida, and the land of Georgia, and the land of the Carolinas, and the land of Virginia,

4. And Abraham proclaimed that the slaves of the tribes in rebellion should be free, and that the armies of the North maintain the freedom of them.

5. And Abraham enjoined upon the Ethiopians, that they should do no violence to any man, except in necessary self-defense.

6. And Abraham further declared that the Ethiopians, who were freed, should be received into armed

service of the State, to garrison forts and positions and stations, and to man vessels of all sorts.

7. And Abraham invoked the considerate judgment of mankind, and the gracious favor of Almighty God, on the edict which he had written.

8. Now the number of Ethiopians that were made free by the edict of Abraham was three millions and one hundred and nineteen thousand and three hundred and four score and ten souls.

9. Therefore there was great rejoicing in the loyal North, and the Ethiopians gathered together in great meetings.

10. And there was shouting and singing and speech-making, and the beating of drums and the firing of cannon.

11. And many cheers were given for Abraham, and for Horace, and for Garrison, and for Cheever.

12. And many contrabands went up to the temples and gave thanks and sang praises.

13. And one arose in the midst of the temple, and lifted up his voice and prayed, saying,

14. "We 'seech thee, O Lord! to 'member de

Union army, support dem on de right and left to carry on dy work;

15. Go before dem like de burning lamp. 'Member de President, de sea sailors and de lan' trabblers; 'member me de meanest ob dem all.

16. Write us a ticket, oh Lord, an' gib us free admission to heabeen. Amen."

CHAPTER LXVIII.

GREENBACKS.

1. When Abraham and his counsellors knew how great was the expense of the war, and how the gold and treasure of the nation were spent, and that much money was needed to pay the soldiers and the sailors and the artificers and the husbandmen and the shoulder-strappers.

2. A wise man named Salmon arose and said, Father Abraham and all ye counsellors, behold I had a dream, and the spirit of the Lord enlightened me, and revealed unto me what should be done, and if ye will I will recount unto you this heavenly direction.

3. Then Abraham said with a loud voice, Salmon, speak on, and the counsellors said, Amen.

4. Then Salmon opened his mouth and spake:

5. Lo, in the depths of the night a new intelligence was given unto me, so that I understood divine sayings

6. And a voice called unto me, saying, Salmon, Arise, get thee into the District of Columbia, and cause to be engraved many likenesses both of Abraham and of thyself.

7. And let the likenesses be printed on strong papers about seven inches and a half long and about three inches and a quarter wide.

8. And let there be engraved also and printed on the papers figures and marks, and letters and signs and symbols, so that no man can make any thing like unto them.

9. And let the name of Chittenden be printed on each paper, and the name also of Spinner in characters that no man can read and no man can write.

10. And let these papers be printed with green ink, and let them be called greenbacks.

11. And the greenbacks shall stand for value, and be taken in payment for debts, and shall represent the nation's credit.

12. And whosoever refuseth to take the greenbacks for payment of debt or to acknowledge their value, let him be unto you an outcast and a traitor.

13. Now when Salmon ceased speaking, the wise

men and elders counselled together, even the wise men of the mighty Sanhedrim,

14. And resolved that it should be as Salmon had dreamed.

15. And they caused to be printed many likenesses of Abraham and of Salmon.

16. And caused to be engraved also and printed on the papers figures and marks, and letters and signs and symbols, so that no man could make any thing like unto them.

17. And caused the name of Chittenden to be printed on each paper, and the name also of Spinner in characters that no man could read and no man could write.

18. And behold these papers were made and printed even as the Lord had directed Salmon in the dream, and they were called also greenbacks.

CHAPTER LXIX.

NORTHERN PROSPERITY.

1. Now when the greenbacks were scattered to the East and to the West, and to the North and to the South,

2. And came into the hands of any man who would labor, that he might buy food and raiment.

3. Behold great was the prosperity of the land, and glad were the hearts of the people.

4. For even as the red blood of the heart giveth health to the body, making the limbs move with joy and the eye beam with gladness,

5. So ran the rich steams of wealth through the Nation, giving new life to business and new zest to pleasure.

6. For cities grew and waxed very great, and the land was overflowing with fatness.

7. And the people said, surely they of the South were false prophets who foretold that grass should grow in the streets of the Queen City.

8. For we have been up and down through the streets thereof, even from Front street to Brighton, and from Mill Creek unto Pendleton.

9. But nary blade of grass could we see in the streets and nary house vacant.

10. But the noise of building is heard in every square, and no one in the whole city sitteth idle.

11. The stalls of the merchants are filled with rich stuffs, and the ladies are dressed in silks and fine linens.

12. The hands of the artificer are busy, the teacher gathereth many to hear the voice of his instruction, and the Priests speak unto mighty congregations.

13. Sing, oh ye people! and let not the voice of thanksgiving be withheld, for great is the prosperity of the nations, and mighty is the power thereof.

CHAPTER LXX.

NEGRO TROOPS.

1. Now after the edict of Abraham had gone out, many Ethiopians fled from the land of Dixie, and came and took refuge in the tents of Abraham.

2. And arms were put into their hands, and captains were placed over them, who should set them in battle array, and lead them against the Rebels, even against those who had been their masters.

3. Now when the Ethiopians heard this they feared not, but they scratched in the midst of the wool which groweth upon the crown of their heads.

4. And the white of their eyes shone like unto snow in the night, or like unto an onion that hath been newly pealed.

5. Now many laughed when the rulers sent forth the Ethiopians, and they said surely this is a good joke,

for are not the contrabands a race of cowards, how then shall they contend with the chivalry of Dixie?

6. Nevertheless it came to pass that the Ethiopians fought bravely, and overcame even the chivalry and put them to shame.

7. So that those who had laughed look grave, and said, truly are the Ethiopians a valiant people, and so we have always thought.

8. Of a truth they fight even as tigers, and that this would be so we have always declared.

9. Now when Jefferson knew that the Ethiopians were in arms against the Rebels, his wrath was kindled mightily, and he sent forth spiteful words, even as a rocket sends forth fire.

10. And he made many terrible threats that the Ethiopians might be frightened, and cease from troubling the Rebels.

11. But the Ethiopians heeded not Jefferson for his much speaking, but each man loaded his musket and did grin.

12. And whatsoever Secesh came in their way they 'went for,' and whomsoever they went for they "gobbled."

13. Now many Ethiopians went out on the gunboats, and many were armed with spades and with shovels, and did build walls and make strong fortresses for a defense against the Rebels.

CHAPTER LXXI.

RUNNING THE BLOCKADE.

1. Now wars increased and multiplied greatly, so that there was no day passed that there was not a skirmish or a battle.

2. And many were the fights by sea and upon the rivers, for great vessels of war were upon the deep and upon the rivers of water.

3. Strong fortresses were builded upon the shores of the rivers, and mighty engines of war were placed thereon, even great cannon.

4. So that no boat could pass up or down, lest they should be demolished and sunken, for the noise of the cannon was like unto thunder, and the stroke of its ball like unto the thunder-bolt.

5. Now there were strong fortifications upon the Father of Waters, even round about the city of Vicksburg, and there were great cannon placed thereon.

6. And there was a boat, the name whereof was the Queen of the West, and Colonel Ellet was the commander of it.

7. Now the crew of the Queen of the West were brave and not fearful, and the commander said, Let us sail by the batteries that are upon the shore, even by the strong forts of Vicksburg.

8. And it was done according as Ellet had spoken, but after this, was the vessel taken by the Rebels.

9. And there was another gunboat, the name of which was the Indianola, and the name of the commander was Brown.

10. And it came to pass, that a certain Admiral, who is called Porter, said unto Brown, Thou also mayst pass the batteries of Vicksburg, even as did Ellet the Colonel.

11. Now Brown did as Porter had commanded, and as the Indianola went past, lo! eighteen guns were fired upon her from the batteries of the Rebels, but no harm came unto her.

12. But it came to pass that the Indianola was captured, and fell into the power of the Rebels.

13. Now Porter had seen that while the vessels of the North were sailing by the batteries of Vicksburg, that five of the great guns of the enemy exploded in firing.

14. Therefore Porter said, I will make a boat in the likeness and the image of a Monitor.

15. And the foundation thereof shall be an old coal barge, and for smoke stacks she will have pork barrels piled one upon another, and for quarter boats two old canoes.

16. And her furnaces shall be of mud, and shall send forth black smoke and not steam.

17. And peradventure when I shall have made this vessel and pushed it into the stream, and it shall float by the batteries, they will fire also upon it, and burst other guns.

18. Now Porter did even as he had thought in his heart, and behold when the boat which he had made floated away,

19. The batteries of Vicksburg opened with a mighty din, so that the earth trembled, and the shot fell thick as the leaves in the Autumn.

20. But the false Monitor escaped unharmed, and

GREAT REBELLION. 259

sailed on and came nigh unto the place where the Indianola was.

21. Now when the Rebels who had taken the Indianola saw the boat coming, they were sore afraid, and cried out, Lo, a turreted monster cometh.

22. And they said, let us destroy the Indianola that she be not recaptured, and let us sail away with all haste, for full surely will destruction come upon us.

23. For of a truth there is no escape from a turreted monster, and in swift flight alone is there a shadow of safety.

24. So they destroyed the Indianola by powder and by fire, and escaped away out of the reach of the turreted monster.

CHAPTER LXXII.

BREAD RIOTS.

1. Now there was great destitution in the land of Dixie, for many of the fields were laid waste, and merchantmen brought no supplies from afar for fear of the ships that Abraham had sent upon the sea.

2. And there arose a famine in the land, and the famine was grievous unto the people, so that they clamored for bread,

3. Saying unto the Rulers and the rich men, give us to eat or we perish, both we and our little ones.

4. And they arose in many cities, and cried out mightily, saying, we will have whereof to eat.

5. Now Richmond was a proud city, and full of sin, even like unto Babylon of old, or like unto the cities of the plain.

6. For, in that city, Jefferson had his throne, and his wicked ministers dwelt there.

7. And some said, surely, Richmond is the main gates of Hell, and the black entrance thereof; but others said, nay, of a truth, Charleston is the main gate, but Richmond is the trap-door that leadeth unto darkness, and unto the place of brimstone.

8. And the famine prevailed in Richmond, and the poor arose, crying for bread, saying, give unto us meat this day, or we perish.

9. And about three hundred women gathered themselves together in the streets, and seized bread, and meat, and flour, and whatsoever was good for food, or for clothing.

10. Now, when the stores were fast closed, and the windows barred, and the doors bolted with strong bolts,

11. The women seized axes, and hatchets, and broke the doors, and burst the bars asunder, and entered in the houses, and did eat, and gave unto their little ones.

12. Then came forth the City Guard, with fixed bayonets, and threatened the women, and said, if ye go not to your homes, ye shall surely die.

13. And they laughed at the Guard, and answered,

saying, hunger cuts more keenly than a knife, and starvation is sharper than a bayonet.

14. Then arose the Governor of the tribe of Virginia, even Governor Letcher, who was a mighty man, and had not tasted hunger.

15. And he reviled those that were hungry, saying, it is a shame unto you, and a disgrace unto the city. Go ye, therefore, unto your houses, and what matter is it if ye be hungry. What is hunger? Hunger hurteth not me. Ye are fools, and sinful, that ye complain of this thing.

CHAPTER LXXIII.

VANCE'S APPEAL.

1. Now there was great want in the land of North Carolina, insomuch that the people feared starvation.

2. And the Governor of the people of that land, who dwelt in the Capital City, even in the City of Raleigh, sent forth a message to the planters of the land,

3. Saying, lo! provisions fail so that there is little to eat, and none to spare, for many have consumed our substance, but there is none to replenish.

4. Without bread the soldier hath neither strength nor courage, and how shall our armies subsist unless we send them provisions.

5. The sword and the spear are a defense against the Yankees, but against the famine who can contend?

6. Plant ye, therefore, and sow, that in due time ye may gather an abundant harvest, that starvation come

not upon us, and our armies disband, because of fierce hunger.

7. But plant ye no cotton, and no tobacco, for these things are not to be eaten.

8. Let no man sow that he may reap great gain unto himself, but that he may save the land from destruction.

9. And let the magistrates see that no one useth the grain for distilling, but let it be made into bread for the starving.

10. And let none take food by violence, for he who breaketh the law gaineth not bread, but much sorrow.

11. And finally, oh Planters, I advise that ye gather yourselves together in council and determine what is best, that ye may act wisely.

12. Now when the Governor had written this appeal he sent it forth to the tillers of the fields, and to all the people.

13. And the people mourned, saying, how sad is our case, and how greatly have sorrows increased in our midst.

14. Verily, the hand of God is against us, and surely the sins of our Rulers rise up in judgment against us.

15. O, that we were as in the days of our prosperity, that we might rest neath the protecting wings of the Union.

16. For now we go forth with sorrow in the morning, and at night we return to our dwellings with weeping,

17. And the remembrance of the days that are gone cometh upon us, and we sigh for the day of peace, and the day wherein we shall be joined to the Northland, and when the North and the South shall be one people.

CHAPTER LXXIV.

FORT SUMTER BOMBARDED.

1. Now when many war vessels had been made ready and clad in iron, and armed with mighty cannon and manned by the bravest of the sons of the North.

2. Behold Dupont goeth forth by the coasts of the South, and leadeth a squadron against the strong fortresses that are over against Charleston.

3. And these are the names of the vessels that were equipped for the fight, and that Dupont led under the battlements of the strong forts.

4. The Weehawken and the Passiac and the Montaud and the Patapsco and the Ironsides and the Catskill and the Nantucket and the Nahant and the Keokuk.

5. Now all these vessels were of great size and strength, and were clad in ribs of iron, and floated upon the sea like unto huge leviathans.

6. When they came up the harbor, and nigh unto Sumter and near unto the many strong forts and batteries of the Rebels, a furious battle began.

7. Mightily fell the hot storm of battle upon the valiant vessels of iron.

8. One hundred and three score were the cannon balls that fell in one minute, and the balls that were shot by the Rebels were in all three thousand five hundred.

9. And the weight of the balls was some one hundred, and some two hundred, and some three hundred and some four hundred pounds.

10. Now the gunners that were upon the boats were strong men, and naked to the waist and grimed with powder.

11. And they did load the guns with many pounds of powder, and did fire from the port holes of the iron clad boats, and their balls fell upon Sumter like thunderbolts upon a mountain.

12. Now went the Keokuk forth from the rest of the fleet and sailed near unto Sumter, and immediately the guns of the rebels were turned upon her.

13. And tons of iron rattled upon her, and ninety

times was she struck, and nineteen rents were made in her armor of iron.

14. And not until then did the Keokuk withdraw herself from the battle, and as she sailed slowly away she shouted a farewell of fury from the black mouth of her cannon.

15. And the Keokuk sunk in the midst of the sea, and behold all the vessels departed, for they were not able to batter down the strong fortresses of Charleston.

CHAPTER LXXV.

UNION MEETINGS.

1. In those days there were evil spirits abroad in the earth, who took to themselves the forms of men,

2. But because of their likeness unto serpents, they were called Copperheads, and they were a great evil in the land.

3. They were otherwise called Butternuts, and some called them Secession sympathizers, and others called them Anti-war-men.

4. Now when the soldiers, who were in the field heard of these Copperheads, and of their sedition, they were wroth,

5. And sent word unto the faithful who remained at home, that they should rebuke the Copperheads, and if the Copperheads ceased not to hiss they should count them as outcasts and as traitors.

6. So the faithful of the North called great meetings in the chief cities, and wise men arose in the midst of the multitudes, and rebuked the Copperheads,

7. And spake well of the soldiers and of the Captains, and of the deeds of the Sanhedrim,

8. And acknowledged Abraham as the Ruler of the land, and entreated the people to cherish the Union and to love the flag of the Nation.

9. And great multitudes leagued themselves together, and sware unto one another that they would sustain the laws of the Nation, and stand by the army.

CHAPTER LXXVI.

CHANCELLORVILLE.

1. Now Burnside ceased to be commander of the Army of the Potomac, and Joseph, who is also called Hooker, became leader in his place.

2. Now Hooker was a mighty warrior, and had achieved great things, whereof the whole world knew, even so that he was called "Fighting Jo."

3. Now, Jo, said to himself, hath not George striven to conquer the host of Lee, and hath not Burnside once and again gone forth to do this thing.

4. Yet have they failed in this, but I will not fail, for I think I am the one man reserved by Providence to destroy the great army of Lee.

5. So Hooker went forth with a great multitude of soldiers and officers, and crossed over the river Rappahannock, and put the battle in array nigh unto the city which is called Chancellorville.

6. Now Chancellorville is a city of one house, and is distant from Fredericksburg about four leauges.

7. And he sent forth a valiant horseman named Stoneman, with three thousand picked men, and commanded him to ride forth beyond the army of Lee, and to spoil the country, and burn the bridges, and tear up the railways,

8. So that no provisions could be brought to the Rebels from Richmond, and so that the Rebel army would be compelled to fight.

9. Now began a fierce battle, and it continued three days, and many were put to the point of the bayonet, and many were shot.

10. And Hooker and his army withdrew from the fight, and crossed the river, and returned even unto the place from which they had gone forth.

11. Now it was seven days from the time when Hooker started across the Rappahannock, until the time he came back unto the place from which they had gone forth.

12. And Hooker said, lo! I have gained a great victory. But Lee said, also, the victory is plainly unto us.

13. And the people murmured again, and said, old Joe braggeth, but his words come to naught. Give us a man of fewer words to lead our armies to battle.

CHAPTER LXXVII.

STONEMAN'S RAID.

1. Now when Stoneman had gone out, as he had been commanded, to spoil the country of the enemy in the land of Dixie,

2. He rode with great speed, and came near unto the City of Richmond, even within two miles of the City.

3. And the soldiers that were with him scattered themselves to the East, and to the West, and to the North, and to the South,

4. And destroyed bridges, and culverts, and ferries, and wagons, and trains of cars,

5. And broke railroads, and canals, and burned canal-boats, and stations, and store-houses, and supply trains, and depots,

6. And captured horses and mules, and three hundred prisoners of war.

7. And visited many towns, and liberated many Ethiopians, and returned safe unto the place from which they had departed.

8. Now the houses that Stoneman, and the cavalry that was with him, destroyed were one score and two, and the culverts were seven, and the bridges were five.

9. And the wagons that were destroyed were an hundred and one score and two, and the horses captured were two hundred, and the mules one hundred and four.

10. And the towns that the cavalry visited were one score and five, and the Ethiopians liberated were an hundred and two score and ten.

11. Now the Ethiopians rejoiced greatly when they saw the horsemen draw nigh to liberate them, and they cried out, Behold, our deliverers come.

12. And many lifted up their voices and gave thanks that ministers had been sent to deliver them from bondage.

13. Now the land through which Stoneman rode, had been a land of milk and of honey, and in times past it had been full of richness.

14. But the desolation of war had compassed it, and the glory of it had departed.

15. The store of the merchant was empty, and the shop of the workman was like unto a ruin, and the dwelling places of the people were vacant.

16. Men had ceased to go up to the temples to worship, and the fear of famine was in the minds of the people.

17. For the sins of the land had brought all this upon them, that they might repent and turn again unto righteousness.

CHAPTER LXXVIII.

VALLANDIGHAM.

1. Now, chief among the Copperheads, was one Clement, whose surname was Vallandigham, who dwelt in the city of Dayton, in the vale of the River Mad.

2. And Clement was crafty, and full of wiles, and full of all wickedness, insomuch that Lucifer made him chief over all the Copperheads, and ruler over the hosts of the Butternuts.

3. Now it came to pass that Clement went about speaking evil things of Abraham, and of the great Captains that Abraham had placed over the armies.

4. But when Burnside heard these things he was wroth, for he abhorred the name of a traitor, and delighted greatly to bring Copperheads unto sorrow.

5. And Burnside said, verily this Copperhead uttereth seditious words, and lieth unto the people.

6. Moreover, hath he not violated the order which I gave unto the people, even order 38, and shall he not suffer for this thing?

7. Hath not Abraham given all power into my hands, that I shall do whatever thing I please with the Copperheads? how, then, shall this chief of the Butternuts go unpunished?

8. And Burnside called a troop, and commanded them, saying, Go ye into the city of Dayton, which lieth in the vale of the River Mad,

9. And draw nigh unto the house of Clement, the Copperhead, and knock upon the door thereof, and if Clement cometh not out unto ye *go pher* him,

10. And bring him unto the Queen City, that he may answer before me for that which he hath spoken.

11. Now the troop went forth, as they had been commanded, and came unto the dwelling of Clement, and knocked at the door thereof, and said, Come forth.

12. But Clement thrust his head out of the window and spake bitterly, saying, I will not come forth. And he fired upon the troop with his pistol.

13. Then the Captain of the troop remembered that

Burnside had said, If he will not come out, ye shall go pher him.

14. So the Captain gave command unto the troop, and they brake the door, and Clement they went for.

15. And after these things, Clement was tried before a great council in the Queen City, and condemned for his much evil speaking, and Burnside commanded that he should be cast into prison.

CHAPTER LXXIX.

MORE ABOUT CLEMENT.

1. Now when Abraham heard that Clement had been condemned to be cast into prison, he had compassion on him, for Abraham was slow to anger and plenteous in mercy.

2. And Abraham said surely my servant Burnside, hath dealt hardly with Clement, but I will not that Clement be cast in prison, for prison will be grievous unto Clement.

3. 'And peradventure Clement will take cold if he lieth in prison, and if he taketh cold he will feel bad.

4. And perhaps Mrs. Clement will feel bad also, if Clement goeth to prison, and I would not that Mrs. Clement should feel bad.

5. So Abraham commanded that Clement should not be sent to prison, but that he should go into the land of Dixie, and make merry with his brethren.

6. And Clement departed and went into the land of Dixie, and abode there not many days.

7. For his brethren received him not, but said get thee into a ship and go to the Province of Canada, and rest thee under the ægis of the British Lion.

8. And it shall come to pass, that when thou standest on the border, and looketh over into the land of thy nativity, that the people of thy State shall say unto thee, Come and rule over us.

9. Now Clement believed what his brethren spake unto him, and he entered into a ship and set sail, and came unto the Province of Canada, and sat down under the British Lion's ægis.

10. And Clement sitteth there to this day, looking over the border, and waiteth for the people to say unto him, Come and rule over us.

CHAPTER LXXX.

PORT GIBSON.

1. Now Ulysses overcame the Rebels in every conflict, and went against them like a devouring flame.

2. And thousands flocked unto the standard of his army, and followed him into the battle, and his praise was in the mouths of the multitude.

3. Now Ulysses went forth with power and with might, to conquer the strongholds of Vicksburg, and to enter the city, and to take captive those that were therein.

4. But he came upon an army of Rebels, nigh unto a place called Port Gibson, and he set the battle in array against them.

5. And it was about the eighth hour, and the fight continued all that day, and it was fierce and bloody.

6. And of the Rebel force there were eleven thousand men, who drew sword, and who fired gun, and of those

a great multitude were killed, and wounded, and many were also taken captive.

7. And of the army of Ulysses not many were slain, but the soldiers rejoiced in the battle, and followed after the Rebels with might and with valor.

8. But the Rebels fled, and came unto Vicksburg, and took refuge within the strong forts of the city.

9. And Ulysses following after, pitched upon the plains to the south of the city, and gathered a mighty force unto him,

10. That he might besiege the place, and bring the inhabitants thereof to starvation.

11. About this time the forts of Grand Gulf were captured, for the war vessels of the North came against them.

12. Now in these days there was great hope in the army of the North, and the Chief Priest, and the rulers, and officers, and the people, thought surely the end of the Rebellion draweth nigh.

13. Yet they knew not that great battles were yet to be fought, and that many days of affliction were yet to be numbered.

CHAPTER LXXXI.

JOHN BULL AND LOUIS NAPOLEON.

1. Now Jonathan was the genius that ruled the destinies of the Yankee Nation, and unto him was given all power, so that even Abraham himself was his subject.

2. And Jonathan took to wife a goddess, even the Goddess of Liberty, who weareth the starry banner, and ruleth with heavenly justice.

3. And Liberty bare unto Jonathan Industry, and Intelligence, and Wealth, and Population, and Free Speech, and Religion, and many other sons and daughters.

4. Now it came to pass that John, whose surname is Bull, and who dwelleth over the sea, and presideth over the destinies of the British, saw the warfare among the people of Jonathan

5. He opened his mouth and roared unto Jonathan, saying, "Hit his himpossible, oh Johnathan, to conquer such hexcellent harmies."

6. But Jonathan answered, and said unto John, Of a truth, nothing is impossible with us, my dear fellow, for verily that is a word unknown to us Yankees.

7. Then cometh the Emperor of the French unto John, and boweth a low bow, and stroketh his moustache, and sayeth,

8. Let us speak unto Jonathan, and command him that he withdraw his armies from enforcing the Rebels, for truly my people and thine are in great need of cotton, and of divers things from the Land of Dixie.

9. But how shall we obtain these things, while Jonathan permitteth Abraham to blockade the ports of the ocean, and prevent the ships that they can not come forth unto us

10. Moreover, is not Jefferson near unto thee, and doth not thy soul yearn to protect him and his people.

12. Then answered John, Thou speakest true, oh Louis, but peradventure when we speak hunto Johnathan 'e will not 'ear us, but hanswer us shortly, hand tell us to 'tend to our business.

14. Louis answered, and said, If he do th s we will join together our war ships, and go forth, and compel him that he do this thing, even as we desire.

15. Then John raiseth up his hands and cryeth, Verily, Louis, thou knowest not what thing thou adviseth, for as my soul liveth, I would not contend with the Yankee.

16. For his gunboats are powerful, and his cannon are 'orrid, and there is no hinfernal hinstrument that he 'ath not hinvented.

17. I remember his strength in the days of his childhood, and I cannot forget him in the days of his manhood.

18. Now when Louis heard the words of John, he was much disappointed, and before he departed he spake once more, saying,

19. If thou wilt not join me in this thing, oh John, let me entreat thee at least to promise that thou wilt yield no sympathy unto Jonathan, but let thy love be rather unto Jefferson, who is our friend.

20. And John promised with many oaths that he would love Jefferson, and hate Jonathan. And he did according as he had promised.

21. Howbeit, Jonathan cared little, but said unto himself, If John wisheth to love Jefferson he may, but if John intermeddleth with the plans that I have made,

22. Perhaps I may sail over the ocean with a small fleet, even a few of the gunboats that I have made.

23. And, peradventure, I will carry away the Island whereon John dwelleth, and cause it to be set down in the place of Virginia, which hath become desolate.

24. So who knoweth, but that in the hands of Providence and myself, England may be turned from the ways of the heathen, and learn to follow after righteousness.

CHAPTER LXXXII.

GRIERSON'S SPLENDID RIDE.

1. Now there was a brave Colonel, whose name was Grierson, who was a commander of five hundred horsemen.

2. And all these were valiant men, who feared no danger, but rejoiced in the din of war, and in the peril of conflict.

3. Now Grierson called unto his men with a loud voice, and said, Let us go down into the midst of the Land of Dixie, even through the heart of Mississippi.

4. And let us destroy the stores of the Rebels, and lay waste their fields, and cut up their railways, and do all manner of harm unto them, for they are our enemies.

5. Now when the horsemen heard this they were glad, and sprang each man to his saddle, saying,

6. Lead us whithersoever thou wilt, for we will follow, and we will obey the words of thy voice.

7. And they rode in sixteen days, even from La Grange, which is in the land of Tennessee, to Baton Rouge, which is in the land of Louisiana, and the whole distance was one score and nine leagues.

8. And they destroyed many bridges, and culverts, and trains of cars, and depots, and locomotives, and railroads, and telegraphs, even as Stoneman had done in the land of Virginia.

9. And when they drew nigh unto the river Pearl they made great haste, that they might come unto the bridge and cross over, for they feared the Rebels would destroy the bridge, for it was rumored that the Yankees were in the land.

10. Now when they came unto the bridge, behold, the pickets of the Rebels had begun to tear the bridge, but the horsemen drove them away, and quickly repaired the bridge, and passed over in safety.

11. And they said, Surely the good Providence brought us to the bridge in time, that we should accomplish that whereunto we are commanded.

12. Now, on the twenty-seventh day of the month,

and about the seventh hour, they came to a certain ferry, but they could not cross the ferry, for the boat was on the other side of the stream.

13. Then came down one of the tribe of Carolina, and spake unto them in the language of Dixie (for he knew not that they were Yankees), and asked if they would cross over.

14. And one spake to the Carolinian, and answered him in his own language, saying, Behold, we are of the tribe of Alabama, and we would that thou shouldst send thy boat hither, that we may cross, even to the other side.

15. Now the Carolinian was deceived, and he caused the boat to be brought over, and they did enter into the boat and cross over, every man.

16. After this came five-and-thirty of the soldiers of Grierson, unto a place which is called Newton.

17. Now the Captain over the five-and-thirty was a brave man, and fear had not entered into his heart.

18. And this Captain said, Lo! I will go unto this town and make its people captive. And he went up boldly and demanded the town, that they should surernder unto him in the name of Grierson, the Colonel.

19. Now, behold, there were three thousand Rebel soldiers in that place, howbeit, the Captain knew it not at the first.

20. So when the Commander of the Rebels said, Give us an hour that we may consider. The Captain replied, An hour I cannot give thee until I have counselled with the reserve,—them first must I see.

21. And the Captain and those that were with him went away hastily, and returned, not that they might take the city, for they desired not to take captive three thousand Rebels.

22. And the reserve of which the Captain had spoken was not, for the words he had used were a ruse by which he might escape.

CHAPTER LXXXIII.

GRAND CHARGE ON VICKSBURG.

1. Now on the twenty-second day of the fifth month, which is called May, Ulysses commanded all his Generals that they should advance upon the city of Vicksburg, and storm it.

2. And he wrote also to David, the servant of Gideon, that he should also fire upon the city with the mighty cannon of his gunboats.

3. For David was Admiral of the Squadron of the Mississippi, and commanded the vessels that guarded the waters of the great River.

4. Now when the third hour had come, there was a terrible onset, and from that hour the noise of battle was like unto thunder.

5. As the lion springeth upon his prey, so rushed the hosts of Ulysses upon the strong walls of the Rebels.

6. And the clashing of swords was heard in the midst of the conflict, and the bursting of shells and the booming of cannon.

7. And the voice of command rose o'er the din of the battle, urging the valiant heroes to break down the walls of the Rebels, and lay waste the strongholds of Vicksburg.

8. And the gunboats of David ceased not to trouble the city, but sent forth from their great guns their swift balls of destruction.

9. But when the evening had come, behold, Vicksburg was not yet taken, and Ulysses commanded that the soldiers should withdraw them from the fight.

10. And a great multitude had fallen in the battle, so that sorrow was great in the tents of Ulysses.

11. And when the darkness of the night came on the rain fell, and gloom overshadowed the hearts of the soldiers, so that many lifted up voices of lamentation and mourning.

12. And some were faint hearted and full of fear, and desired to depart away from before the strong city, for they hoped not that they should finally triumph.

13. But Ulysses was stout of heart, and spake cheer

fully unto the soldiers, and said, Lo! though we have not yet taken this stronghold of traitors,

14. Yet will we surely prevail if ye have patience and valor, for now am I determined to lay siege to the city.

15. And as my soul liveth, I will not abandon this work until Pemberton yieldeth, and until the city acknowledge that we are stronger than they.

16. Now while Ulysses continued to lay siege to the city of Vicksburg, Nathaniel, who is also called Banks, drew nigh unto a place which is called Port Hudson.

17. Now Port Hudson was a stronghold of the Rebels, and was upon a high place, even upon the banks of the Father of Waters, like unto the stronghold of Vicksburg.

18. And Nathaniel set his army in array against the batteries of the Rebels, and the charge of the soldiers was like unto the sweep of the whirlwind.

19. And many gunboats also fired upon the forts from the River; for an Admiral, who is called Farragut, had come up that he might assist Nathaniel.

20. But when the battle had lasted many days, the

strong place had not fallen, and Nathaniel did even as Ulysses had done at the city of Vicksburg.

22. For Nathaniel saw that the strong place could not be taken by assault, but that surely it would yield to the power of hunger.

CHAPTER LXXXIV.

ARBITRARY ARRESTS.

1. Now it came to pass that when Clement had been arrested and many others both of the race of Copperheads and Butternuts.

2. Because of their much speaking against Abraham and the acts that he had done, and because of the words which they said against joining the army.

3. That a great multitude of Democrats were gathered together, even at the capital of the land of New York, which is called the Empire State.

4. And when they had assembled themselves they appointed from their number some of the wisest who should write Resolutions.

5. Now these wise ones went out and wrote many sayings, and returned unto the meeting, and read all that they had written.

6. And the multitude were well pleased with the writing of the wise men, and they lifted up their voices and with one accord shouted "Bully."

7. Now the sayings that the wise men had written in the Resolutions were pompous, and like unto those things, which—in the tongue of the vulgar—are gassy.

8. And the wise men professed much love for the nation, nevertheless they said many hard things of works that Abraham had done, blaming him because he had permitted Clement to be arrested.

9. For they said, truly Clement did not any overt thing, but spake only words of truth and soberness concerning Abraham and Burnside, neither did he do any treason.

10. Which things are also proper to be spoken, for Daniel the Prophet hath said, surely "it is the ancient and undoubted prerogative of this people to canvass public measures and the merits of men."

11. Now when the wise men had written these Resolutions, and many speeches had been made, they sent a letter unto Abraham, and enclosed therein the Resolutions.

12. When Abraham received the letter, he replied

unto the wise men, with words of honesty and candor, and showed the deceit of their hearts and their flimsy pretenses.

13. For Abraham had searched the Scriptures and knew well how to take the crafty in his own net as well as to answer the fool according to his folly.

CHAPTER LXXXV.

DEATH OF JACKSON.

1. Now in the midst of the battles on the river Rappahannock, fell Jackson, who was also called Stonewall, for he was like unto a bulwark and a strong defense unto his people.

2. And there was none like unto him in all the land of the Rebels, for he was a just man and feared God and obeyed his commandments.

3. Only in one thing did he sin against Heaven, and in one thing did the voice of the Evil One allure him.

4. For he heard not the Gospel which commandeth to open the doors of the prison, and to let the captive go free.

5. Nevertheless when he departed away out of the land of the living, his praise was in the mouth of all

people, both those whom he had led on to the battle and those with whom he contended.

6. And the people in the land of the South mourned many days, putting on sackcloth and ashes, and weeping sorely for the loss of their leader,

7. Crying aloud in the streets, who is like unto Jackson, and where shall we seek for another like unto him.

8. For great was his skill, and his courage was as the courage of a lion; swift was he to pursue the foe but great was his love to his brethren.

9. Now after this there was great despondency in the armies of the Rebels, for they found no leader like unto Jackson.

10. And about this time there was a season of rest in all the armies, both of the Union and of Rebeldom,

11. Except in the Army of Ulysses, which rested not, but labored both by day and by night to overthrow the strong walls of Vicksburg.

12. But the Army of Rosecrans moved not in the land of Tennessee, and all remained quiet on the River Potomac.

CHAPTER LXXXVI.

LEE INVADES PENNSYLVANIA.

1. Now after all the armies had been quiet for many days, and the people began to inquire, one of another, What meaneth this great silence.

2. Behold, there came a rumor that Lee had crossed over the River Potomac into the borders of the land of Maryland, and of the land of Pennsylvania.

3. And great fear fell upon the people, and upon the President, and the governors, and the captains, and the horsemen, and the foot-soldiers.

4. And people gathered together at the corners of streets, and in all manner of places, and did frighten one another with horrible reports.

5. And said, Who knoweth but that these Rebels will put us all to the edge of the sword, and consume our substance, and destroy our habitations, and eat up our children, and dig the bones of the pilgrim fathers from their graves, and burn them?

6. Who knoweth what city shall first fall into their hands, whether Harrisburg, or Philadelphia, or Washington, or New York, or Boston?

7. Happy is Henry Ward, who saileth over the ocean, for surely would he speedily perish by the hands of these Rebels.

8. Woe now unto Horace, and Wendell, and Cheever, and woe unto those who write for the "Atlantic."

9. Woe unto the Priests of the "New York Independent," and unto all who preach the doctrines of Emancipation.

10. Thus cried the people in their fright and in their great consternation, but the Copperheads rejoiced and were glad, for they loved the Rebels.

11. And John Bull laughed a mighty laugh, and thought, Surely the signs of the times are bright, for if the Rebels shall begin to prevail over Jonathan, then will I do as Louis hath advised, and go to fight with the Yankees.

12. But not until the danger is well nigh passed will I go, for I have no pleasure in thoughts of a battle with Jonathan.

CHAPTER LXXXVII.

THE CALL FOR MILITIA.

1. When Abraham knew that the Rebels drew nigh unto the cities of the North, he straightway wrote an edict,

2. Calling upon the people that they should send forth men to the defense of the Nation.

3. And the number of souls that Abraham desired was one hundred thousand, who should hasten with all speed to repel the invader.

4. From the land of Maryland ten thousand, and from the land of West Virginia ten thousand, and from the land of Ohio thirty thousand, and from the land of Pennsylvania fifty thousand.

5. And Abraham declared that these should be mustered forthwith into the army, and be armed, and equipped, and prepared for battle in no time, and serve for six months in volunteer service.

6. And on the same day that Abraham sent forth his edict, so also did the Ruler of the tribes of Pennsylvania send forth his edict, so also did David, who was Ruler of the tribes of Ohio, send forth his edict, and so also did many others send forth their edicts.

Furthermore, Abraham said, Surely things can not prosper unless the Chief Captain of the Army of the Potomac is changed, for lo! it hath been more than a week since my servant Hooker hath been Chief Captain.

8. So Abraham caused Meade to be Chief Captain in the place of Joe, whose surname is Hooker.

9. And it was heralded to and fro in the land that Meade had been made Chief Captain over the great Army.

10. Now when the people read in the Dailies that Abraham had made Meade to be Chief Captain, they said, Who is this man, and whence cometh he? Verily, we know not the name?

11. But when they read the pretty sayings that Meade had written when he became Chief Captain, and knew the modesty of his words, and that he boasted not as Joe had boasted,

12. They said, Peradventure, he will do much better than Joe—and if he do not, verily he will not do less than George.

13. So they were satisfied, and all men prophesied that Meade should do mighty works, and, peradventure, drive the Rebels out with great slaughter, and free the tribes of the land of Pennsylvania, and of the land of Maryland, from devastation and from ruin.

CHAPTER LXXXVIII.

THE K. G. C.

1. When it had been commanded by Abraham, and by the great Sanhedrim, that a great conscription should take place, and that officers should go about and enroll the names of the young men of the land,

2. Both those that had taken to themselves wives, and those who had not yet come to the years of wisdom and discretion, but had reached a certain age.

3. Behold, many banded themselves together, saying, We will not give our names to these men, and we will not enroll ourselves in the army of the North.

4. So they went about to kill those who had been appointed to enroll the names of the young men.

5. And some they slew secretly, and others they fell upon with a mighty power, and with great numbers, and murdered.

6. Now they who had thus banded themselves together called themselves Knights, even Knights of the Golden Circle, and they said, We will not serve our country, nor respect the laws thereof.

7. Now the Knights of the Golden Circle were of the race of Copperheads, and of the tribes of the meanest Butternuts.

8. And they dwelt in the low places of the South of the land of Hoosiers, which is called the Pocket.

9. And in the darkness of Egypt, which is in the South, of the land of the Suckers,

10. And in divers provinces and towns, where whiskey aboundeth, and the light of knowledge hath not dawned.

11. Now there was one Oliver, whose surname was Morton, who was Chief Ruler of the land of the Hoosiers.

12. And Oliver was a just man, and ruled his people wisely, and loved God, and eschewed the Butternuts.

13. And a great feud arose between Oliver and the Knights, and it came to pass that Oliver's wrath was kindled against the Knights, and he caused many of

them to be seized and dealt with according to their sins.

14. And Lewis, also, who is called Wallace, sought after the Knights, that he might slay them, for Lewis was not to be fooled with.

15. And Burnside, also, continued after this vicious people, like unto a stick that is sharpened; and it came to pass that the Copperheads entered into their holes, and the Knights became scattered.

CHAPTER LXXXIX.

GOOD WORKS.

1. It came to pass that, when many of the soldiers of the Armies of the North had sickened of divers diseases, or were prostrated from the wounds which they received in battle.

2. So that the Hospitals were filled with the suffering, and the pestilence walked in the midst of the camps,

3. The people of the North gathered themselves together in meetings and counselled one with another, devising how they should give comfort unto their brethren who suffered.

4. And they called these meetings, "Soldiers' Aid Meetings," because they were held for the good of those who suffered in war.

5. Now the Soldiers' Aid Societies grew and multiplied exceedingly, and were established in every village and town and city of the land.

6. And they collected together provisions of all kinds, and soft clothing and bandages to bind up wounds, and healing salves to anoint the sores of the wounded.

7. All these things they sent forth to the camps, and the fields of battle, and the hospitals, and to whatsoever places the sufferers were.

8. Moreover, they sent books that the soldiers might read, and papers to gladden their hearts, and many letters full of glad tidings from home, and of cheerful sayings.

9. Now foremost in all good works were the churches, for they remembered the teachings of Him who went about to do good.

10. And many who before had reviled the churches, saying, "they are filled with hypocrisy and all manner of sin, were inclined kindly unto them, and forgot their former bitterness.

11. For they saw that the churches followed after the true spirit of righteousness, and did those works

of goodness and brotherly love, which the Scripture commandeth.

12. But none of the works of love that were done were like unto the toils of the women, for they ceased not night nor day to do deeds of compassion and patience.

13. And men said, Behold the marvellous works of love that woman hath done. Let us speak her name with reverence, and let her character be lifted up in the Nation.

CHAPTER XC.

SPECULATION.

1. Now great multitudes departed from the worship of the true God, and fell down and worshipped Mammon.

2. And some offered up unto this false God, Honor, and Conscience, and Good Faith, and Country.

3. And many waxed rich, even on the sorrows of the people, and did coin gold, even from the blood of the soldier.

4. And many who were in high places sought how they might receive great gain, by the selling of honor.

5. And the temple of Mammon was set up, even in the midst of the Capitol City, and the statue of Mammon rose above the statue of Liberty, which standeth on the dome of the Capitol.

6. And the great Rulers said, Behold, are not all

corrupt, and shall we not also become corrupt,—are we better than other men, or why should we forbear to do sin for the sake of a mere name?

7. So it came to pass that the Rulers were corrupted by their own evil thoughts, and they who were ruled were corrupted by their masters.

8. For the Rulers are the head of the fountain, and the People are the stream, and if the head of the fountain is corrupt, how shall the stream be pure?

9. Give ear, oh! Extortioners, and all ye who buy that ye may sell again, and greatly multiply your profits.

10. For the day cometh when your ill-gotten gain shall perish out of your hands, and the sweetness of the cup of richness shall be bitter as the apples of Sodom.

11. For the eye of Justice sleepeth not, and the ear of God heareth the secret bargain that ye make in the cunning of your deceit.

12. The blood of the slain cryeth to Heaven from the field of battle, and the moan of the hungry pierceth the ear of the Just One.

13. Rejoice in fruit of your falsehood, and buy wine with the wealth ye have stolen, but hope not for visits from Angels, or sweet meditations with Heaven.

CHAPTER XCI.

PRIVATEERING.

1. Now Gideon was the Chief Ruler over the Navies of the land of Jonathan, and under him were placed many Captains, who sailed out upon the the sea in ships,

2. To blockade the coasts of Dixie, and to do battle with the ships of the enemies of Jonathan.

3. And there were also gun boats, of divers forms and curious workmanship; and these guarded the rivers, and the bays, and the coasts of the land.

4. Now the gun boats wear mighty engines of war, and nothing like unto them, had been known before, since the world was.

5. And it was these that made John Bull to fear, for he knew not how he could contend with such monsters of the deep.

6. But, notwithstanding the great ships which Gid-

eon directed, and the mighty iron clad gun boats that had been made, the power of Jonathan prevailed not greatly at sea, as it did upon the land,

7. For many pirates and bold robbers infested the sea, to destroy merchants' ships, and to rob, and to kill.

8. Now chief among the sea robbers, was Raphael, whose surname was Semmes, who had been a servant of Jonathan in the days of old.

9. Now Raphael had joined himself to the cause of the Rebels, and was made Commander of the craft Sumpter.

10. And Raphael did run the blockade, on the River Mississippi, and escaped into the open sea, and followed after merchantmen that were unarmed, and robbed them, and burned them with fire.

11. And the fame of Raphael was spread throughout many lands, and his name became a terror unto those who went out in ships.

12. Now, at length, the Sumpter was taken out of the power of Semmes, but he himself went free, and came to the land of England.

13. And John Bull gave into his hands the ship

Alabama, and Raphael went again to sea, and burned more vessels, even ten whalers, and six merchantmen, and many small trading ships.

14. And the people of Jonathan were sore vexed, that Raphael was permitted to do these things. and they complained much of the Navy, and of the Captains of it.

15. And Gideon was troubled in his spirit, and all the sea Captains and sailors were troubled that they could not take Rapheal, and deal with him according as, in their vengence, they desired.

16. Now there were many other Pirates and Privateers on the sea in those days, and the warfare that they waged, was greater than the warfare of the Regular Navy, over which Gideon did rule.

CHAPTER XCII.

THE FOREIGN ELEMENT.

1. Now the tribes of the land of Jonathan were many, for they were gathered together from all nations, and tongues, and kindreds, and peoples,

2. Even from the uttermost parts of the earth, and from all islands of the sea, and from every land upon which the sun shineth.

3. But chief among the tribes that came from afar were the Celts and the Teutons.

4. Now the Celts were diggers of the earth, and wielded the pick and the shovel, and were much skilled in the making of ditches and the wheeling of barrows.

5. And they bare great love unto all manner of bad whiskey, whether Rot-gut, or Bust Head, or Trip Foot; but they hated the Ethiopian, who, in their language, is called "nayger."

6. And they read not, neither did they write, nor did it enter into their hearts to conceive of the understanding of Law and of Freedom.

7. But they joined hands with the lovers of Clement, and drank much from the jug of the Butternut.

8. Nevertheless, some inclined their hearts unto wisdom, and entered into the counsels of the faithful, and joined themselves unto the armies of Freedom,

9. And went out to the battle, and won unto themselves honor, and glory, and the praise of the people, and the blessing of Heaven.

10. Now the Teutons loved not the Celts, but clave rather unto meerschaums and lager.

11. Yet were they swift unto battle, and loud in the praise of the Radical Captains, and down on slow men and conservative measures.

12. And whatever things were not done according to logic Teutonic, they censured, saying, "Ah, das ist all hoompug."

13. And the Teutons followed diligently the Gospel of John Charles, who is the husband of Jessie; for John was a Radical after the most straitest sect, and Jessie had written "Der Leibgarde."

14. For the Teutons read books, and wrote much, and made speeches; howbeit, some said they know not the American spirit.

15. And surely they imagine a vain thing, when they hope we will forsake all and go "fight mit Sigel."

16. For the Leopard cannot change the color of his spots, nor the man his feelings—and much is plain unto the Teuton, and we *cannot see it*.

CHAPTER XCIII.

THE $300 CLAUSE.

1. Now when the time drew nigh that had been set apart to cast lots to see who of the young men should go forth to the army,

2. Many murmurs arose among the Copperheads, and the Butternuts, and the Traitors, and the Cowards, and those of the Celts who dwelt in the shadow of Clement.

3. And some of the better sort raised the voice of complaint, saying, The statute that the great Sanhedrim hath made is not just,

4. For it provideth that he who shall pay three hundred greenbacks unto the Nation, the same shall be exempted from draft, neither shall he go forth to the battle.

5. Therefore, it will come to pass that the rich will

not go forth, but will pay, every man, his three hundred greenbacks.

6. But the poor man shall go in sadness of heart to the battle, for how shall he give that which he hath not to save him?

7. But the Chief Rulers and the Expounders of the law gave answer, saying, Surely ye do err, not knowing the spirit of the law, which is just unto all men.

8. For the act of Conscription is right and just in all things, sparing the son of the infirm, and the aged, and the widow, and the brother of the orphan.

9. And it is also just, that he who payeth three hundred greenbacks shall be exempted, that the business of the land shall not be broken and injured.

10. For it is needful that some should supply the means whereby the war may continue, and those who labor at home uphold the arm of the soldier who fighteth.

11. Moreover, the money that the Nation obtaineth from him who chanceth to pay for exemption, shall surely be used for the hire of soldiers, for this is the law.

12. And if there is a poor man among ye whom ye think ought not to go forth when he is drafted, but who hath not the greenbacks wherewith he may purchase exemption.

13. Let the friends of such an one join together and pay, each one a portion, and make glad the heart of the poor man and his household.

14. For blessed is he that giveth, and ye should thank the Wise Men of the Sanhedrim that they have made a just law, which enableth you to show forth your good works.

CHAPTER XCIV.

BLACK TROOPS.

1. When the Ethiopians knew that they might go forth, even as a white man goeth, and enter into the army, and fight for the freedom of their people.

2. They waited not, but came with all haste, both those who dwelt in the North, and the contrabands who had been in bondage.

3. And they joined themselves into companies of tens, and of hundreds, and Captains were placed over them.

4. And the troops of the Ethiopians multiplied exceedingly, and they gathered in wrath against the hosts of the Rebels, even as dark clouds gather before a storm breaketh.

5. And the Rebels were enraged greatly when they knew how the Ethiopians gathered against them, for

they had done the Ethiopians wrong, and them they both hated and feared.

6. For they remembered the days of old, even the days of the great Revolution, and the many battles that the Ethiopians had fought;

7. The fights on the Lakes of Champlain and of Erie, and in the land of Florida, and at Schuylkill, and at Horse Shoe Bend, and Pensacola, and New Orleans.

8. And the Rebels sware vengeance on such of the Ethiopians as they should take captive, saying, Let us sell them again into bondage.

9. And they did even as they had sworn, and whatsoever Ethiopian soldier fell captive into their hands they sold into bondage.

10. But if the captive resisted the might of the Rebels, and refused to go into bondage, him they scourged with many stripes, until he yielded submission.

11. And if any captive yielded not submission when he was scourged, him they slew, for their hearts were hardened, even as the heart of Pharaoh.

12. Now when it was known in the North that the

Rebels sold unto bondage the captives that they had taken from among the Ethiopians,

13. And had also scourged them, and put them to death shamefully;—the Rulers of the North said, Verily, these things must not be so.

14. But surely, if these Rebels do this wicked thing to our people, we will visit our vengeance upon them, and do violence to the captives that we have taken from the tribes of the lands of Dixie.

CHAPTER XCV.

EAST AND WEST.

1. Now the Devil spake unto the Copperheads of Egypt and of the Pocket, saying, Behold, ye are foolish and blind that ye cleave unto the Yankees of the East.

2. For, of a truth, the Yankees are well skilled in all manner of subtlety, and they plot against ye that they may gain great power, and rule over you.

3. Seek ye, therefore, to separate yourselves from them, and go not into their counsels any more, but make unto yourselves a distinct nation.

4. And let the nation, that ye shall erect, be called the North-Western Confederacy, and I and my servant Clement will rule over it.

5. Now the Copperheads of Egypt and of the Pocket were pleased with this thing that the Devil had said, and they told it unto the Knights, and the Knights also were well pleased.

6. Then goeth the Devil to the Army of the Cumberland, and saith, Behold, oh soldiers, ye are mostly men of the West, and surely ye desire the prosperity of your country.

7. Seek, therefore, to flee away from your tents and come unto the North-West, and join yourselves unto me, and unto Clement, and the Copperheads, and we will greatly magnify the North-West and create of it a new nation.

8. And we will separate ourselves from the Yankees of the East, who are an abomination unto us.

9. And surely it is a shame unto you also, that ye cleave unto the Yankees, for do they not despise your language and manners, and do they not revile ye in that your boots are not blackened?

10. Moreover, they fight not, but are cowards, and give unto you the heat and burden of the battle, but they themselves take the greenbacks.

11. Come ye, therefore, out from among them, and ye shall have whiskey without money, and without price, and Abraham shall no longer be your Ruler, but I myself will be your leader, and Clement also shall come and assist me.

12. Now when the soldiers heard what the Devil desired, there arose a great swearing, like unto which had not entered into the imagination of the Devil

13. And the curses of the soldiers exploded like bombshells, and fell upon the Devil in hundreds of millions, so that he cried aloud, with a voice like unto thunder,

14. Oh, that I were in the midst of the lake of burning, for the heat of these oaths is worse than fires infernal, and even seven times hotter than the hottest fires of Hades.

15. And after many days, when the Devil recovered, so that he could come again unto the land of Egypt, he crawled in the midst of the Copperheads.

16. And they spake unto him, saying, How is it with thee, Master, and what news bringeth thou from the army.

17. And the Devil was silent, and the Copperheads were sore perplexed, and they spake again unto him, saying, Master, speak unto us, and say how prospereth our cause, and when shall the North-West become a new Nation.

18. Then spake the Devil unto the Copperheads,

Go ye, every one, to his place, for full surely is this new Nation played out.

19. And the Copperheads went away sorrowful, and came each one to his own place, and abode there.

20. But the Devil went to Canada and took lodgings with Clement, even under the ægis of the Lion of Britain.

CHAPTER XCVI.

BATTLE OF GETTYSBURG.—FIRST DAY.

1. Now when the army of the rebels had passed over the river Potomac, and came and sat down at Hagerstown, which is in the land of Maryland:

2 Meade also came forth to meet them at the head of the mighty army of the Potomac,

3. And when Lee, who was the chief captain of the hosts of the Rebels, knew that Meade drew nigh, he commanded his officers that they should lead the soldiers unto the borders of the land of Pennsylvania.

4. And the two mighty armies came together nigh unto Gettysburg, which lieth to the south of the land of Pennsylvania and not far from the mountains that are called Blue Ridge.

5. Now on the first day of the month, July, Reynolds, who led the advance of the army of Meade, came upon the front of the Rebels.

6. And Reynolds commanded his artillery that they should fire upon the Rebels and drive them back that they might feel the might of his power.

7. Then began a fierce battle; and lo Reynolds was slain; for the rifles of the Rebels were deadly.

8. Now when Doubleday, who was also a captain in the army of the north, saw that Reynolds was slain, he took command of the soldiers.

9. And Howard also came to the field and led corps eleventh, which joined battle with the Rebels also and fought with great fury;

10. And the battle raged with great fury, even until nightfall, and the ground was red with the blood of the valiant.

11. Yet had neither array conquered on that day; but the host of the north withdrew to the southward and were set in battle away upon the hill which is called Cemetery.

12. And when midnight drew near Meade came unto the camp of the army and beheld all the line of battle that Howard had made ready for the morrow.

13. And Meade approved of all that Howard had

done, and said it is well, and the host waited on the hill until morning.

14. Now the line of battle which Howard had arranged was in the form of a horse's shoe; and the corps that were in the line were six corps.

15. The corps of Slocum, and the corps of Howard, and the corps of Hancock, and the corps of Doubleday, and the corps of Sickles, and the corps of Sykes.

16. And Meade placed himself in the center of the line, that he might direct the order of battle and that he might the more easily behold the whole of the conflict.

CHAPTER XCVII.

GETTYSBURG.—SECOND DAY.

1. Now when the morning of the second day had fully come, all prepared themselves unto the battle, for strong were the foes that had met, and great was their courage and valor.

2. But the day had well nigh passed, and the evening was at hand when the Rebels came forth to the conflict.

3. Then marched forth Longstreet and Hill, mighty captains of the South, and they led forth forty and five thousand of the bravest of the Rebels.

4. And they moved onward silent and steady, like unto a dark cloud when it moveth up the blue of the Heavens.

5. And they fell mightly upon the corps of Sickles, and forced them back slowly even as a mighty wind driveth a billow.

6. And the noise of the conflict was terrible, and the smoke of the battle was as of the burning of cities, and the ground was heaped with the dead and the wounded and dying.

7. Now came Hancock and Sykes to the aid of the valiant Sickles, and joined the power of their arms to the might of his valor, but on swept the host of the Rebels, and the Northmen regained not their footing.

8. Then came up the Twelfth Corps of Slocum, and the Sixth Corps of Sedgwick, who had come rapidly from far that he might join battle also with the Rebels.

9. For Sedgwick had marched for thirty and six hours, and his soldiers were weary and would fain rest, but when they saw the tide of the battle and how danger threatened the army, they said, "Lead us on to the conflict.

10. And they came down like a whirlwind and drove back the Rebels even to the spot whence they had come forth.

11. Now the battle raged until late in the night, and the victory was to the Army of Meade, for the Rebels were sore beaten and repulsed at all points.

CHAPTER XCVIII.

GETTYSBURG.—THIRD DAY.

1. Now when the morning of the third day had come, the battle was renewed, and on this day the soldiers of Slocum fell upon Ewell, and thus open the conflict.

2. And the charges on both sides were fired, and all the forenoon the hot combat continued, and then the armies rested for a little space.

3. Then began a mighty cannonade, the like of which had not been known in the nation, and it continued three hours, and it was from a hundred of the guns of Lee against the hill whereupon were the hosts of Meade,

4. And now came a great column of Rebels, and the Rebel Chief Armistead led them, and they dashed with great fury towards the brigade of Webb.

5. And when Armistead had halted a moment, that he might put his column in perfect array, so that he could more surely destroy the brigade of Webb.

6. Webb cried with a loud voice unto his soldiers and commanded them that they should charge upon the enemy.

7. And they fell upon the Rebels with fury and killed many, and made Armistead captive, and three thousand of the souls that were with him.

8. Thus the battle was ended, and the victory was to the Army of Freedom, for the hosts of Lee came no more against the Army of the Potomac.

9. And when the night had come the hosts of the Rebels withdrew and fled away toward Virginia, that they might escape away out of the land of the North.

10. Now in the three great battles that were fought at Gettysburg, great numbers were slain, and multitudes were sore wounded.

11. Of the great Chiefs of the army of the North, were slain, Reynolds, and Zook, and Farnsworth, and Weed.

12. And of the great Chiefs of the army of the North, were wounded, Doubleday, and Sickles, and

Hancock, and Butterfield, and Gibbon, and Webb, and Caldwell, and Warren, and Hunt, and Paul, and Barlow, and Meredith, and Graham.

13. Now Lee, when he had fled, came to the River Potomac, and made a bridge, and crossed over into the land of Virginia, and came unto his own place, even the stronghold of Rebels.

14. After these things many Copperheads were turned from darkness into marvellous light, for they had learned that the Rebels of the South respected them not above their neighbors,

15. But plundered both Butternuts and men— neither did they spare the coward, because of his whining.

16. Therefore, in those days flourished War Democrats, and the party of them waxed mighty, and spread through the length and the breadth of the Nation.

CHAPTER XCIX.

BRAGG RETREATS FROM CHATTANOOGA.

1. Now when Rosecrans had been a long time resting with the hosts that were with him, and the people began to wonder, saying, Why goeth he not out against the Rebels.

2. For the army of Bragg had pitched round about Chattanooga, which is a goodly place, lying nigh unto the land of Georgia, and upon the River Tennessee.

3. Behold, there came tidings that the Army of the Cumberland had departed out of their camp, and marched to the southward.

4. And some feared for the army lest it should go too far into the enemies country, and be cut off by Guerrillas.

5. For in those days, Morgan and those who followed him, went about seeking whom they might

devour (for they had not yet came into the land of the Buckeye).

6. But Rosecrans had sent forth spies and scouts, who, mounted on swift horses, and who took heed that no danger should come upon the army suddenly, and that it might not be taken unawares.

7. Now when Rosecrans drew nigh unto Chattanooga, behold, the great host of the Rebels fled to the mountains and sought safety therein from the sword of the pursuers.

8. Howbeit, many were taken captive, and the fame of Rosecrans was spread abroad through the land.

9. Now the armies of the North prospered greatly in these days, and the people rejoiced in the victories which were achieved.

CHAPTER C.

VICKSBURG FALLS.

1. On the day which is called the Sabbath of Freedom, even the Fourth of July, which is sacred unto him who loveth his country,

2. Ulysses looked forth from his tent, and behold one cometh with the white flag of submission, saying, Oh, Ulysses, we can hold out against thee no longer, and I am come from our Chief to ask in his name a favor at thy hands.

3. Then said Ulysses, Speak, and make known the desire of thy Chief, that I may judge of his request, and make answer unto him quickly.

4. Then spake he who had been sent, saying, Our Chief willeth to surrender unto thee if thou wilt permit that his men may march out.

5. Then Ulysses gave answer, Surely no man marcheth out but as a prisoner of war;—this say ye unto him who sent ye;—but if your Chief surrendereth himself and his men as prisoners unto me, no one shall be harmed.

6. After these things, the Chief Captain of the Rebels surrendered both himself and his men prisoners of war unto Ulysses, and they marched out and gave up their arms unto Ulysses.

7. And were paroled, every man, and then they departed away, and were scattered throughout the land of Dixie.

8. And the number of prisoners that Ulysses paroled was about thirty and two thousand souls; and of these were one Lieutenant-General, and four Major-Generals, and twelve Brigadier-Generals.

9. And there were taken also at Vicksburg two hundred pieces of artillery, and forty thousand muskets and rifles, great store of clothing and munitions of war.

10. Now after this Ulysses waited not, but sent forth a force to the assistance of Nathaniel that he might overcome Port Hudson.

11. And Hudson fell also, and many captives were taken, even six hundred thousand souls who drew sword.

CHAPTER CI.

THANKSGIVING PSALM.

1. "Thanks be to God who giveth us the victory," for the arms of our people have triumphed, and the glory of Dixie is laid low.

2. The proud hosts of Lee have been scattered, the stronghold of Vicksburg hath fallen, and the Rebels have fled at Helena.

3. For the Lord has weakened the arm of the Slaver, but he hath given strength to the lover of Freedom.

4. "Oh bless our God, ye people, and make the voice of his praise be heard."

5. Give thanks unto God, oh ye people, for he hath blessed us graciously.

6. Give thanks for brave Captains and soldiers, give thanks for wise Rulers and leaders.

TESTIMONIALS.

I am well acquainted with Dr. Schmucker, the author of the History of the Civil War, and know him to be a man of great mental power. He has attained high reputation in the literary world as a powerful writer.

His History of the Civil War, thus far, is characterized by a lucid, animated and vigorous style. He is clear and yet condensed; happy in his selections and groupings of events.

He has succeeded in giving the reader a full, connected and satisfactory (history) view of the rise and progress of the war.

Those who desire to possess a book on this subject, of permanent value, and at the same time of deep and thrilling interest, should subscribe for the work.—*S. Sprecher, D.D., President of Wittemberg College, Springfield, O.*

The author is well known as a historian of no ordinary merit, and works from his pen of this class have always been popular with the public on account of their reliability. The writer has spared neither time nor labor to acquire the most authentic information in regard to all matters on which he treats, and although an impression seems to exist in the minds of a great many that it is an impossibility to get at the facts in reference to numerous events transpiring around us, in this wicked rebellion, a careful examination of this work will soon dispel all such doubts, and the reader will be satisfied that Dr. Schmucker has overcome all the obstacles which they imagined could possibly intervene, and has written a truthful and impartial history.—*Wilmington Journal, Del.*

From the opening of the Secession guns upon Fort Sumter to the present time, the author gives a succinct account of the war, related with an impartiality that does honor to his genius, and ranks him high among the few capable historians of this country.

The publisher has issued this work from the press in a style that does himself great credit in these days of high prices. The paper, press-work and binding, are unexceptionable; added thereto, are many steel plate engravings, and other illustrations, all enhancing the value of a book published at so low a price. We are sure every one of our readers will at once purchase a copy.—*New York Sun.*

It is a beautiful volume, and handsomely illustrated by plates by Mr. Sartain. Upon examination we find it to contain a well written history of the events of the war, from its beginning until the departure of McClellan's army from the Peninsula, after the battle before Richmond. His description of battles, sieges, &c., are written with a vivid and powerful pen. Indeed, the style of the whole work is remarkable for its extreme force, purity and elegance. We think Mr. Schmucker has here produced a master-piece of historical composition.—*Philadelphia City Item.*

The work is evidently written with much ability, and is the result of careful and extensive research on the part of the author. It possesses the high merit of probing the cause of events, showing the influence of one upon another, and the relation between them. The descriptions of battles are extremely vivid and exciting. The style of the work is a model of elegant and correct composition, and compares favorably with that of the most advanced and popular historians. The biographical sketches of the chief heroes of the war are particularly interesting.—*U. S. Business Journal, Phila.*

The author has evidently been diligent in his pursuit of information from authentic sources. His style of writing is neat and flowing, without attempts at startling effects.—*New York Tribune.*

TESTIMONIALS.—(Continued.)

The work records the events of the present rebellion, while they are vividly impressed upon the public mind, and their true importance and relations best understood.—*Philadelphia Ledger.*

The book has more than ephemeral merit, in being perfectly reliable as to names and dates, so far as we can judge, and gives a fair, impartial account of the war from its inception in the minds of traitors down to the close of the Peninsular campaign.—*New Haven Palladium.*

It is a very comprehensive and correct narrative of the events, both military and civil, which have led to and characterised the rebellion—*Journal and Courier, New Haven, Ct.*

The author has evidently devoted great labor to the production of this volume, carefully condensing a vast amount of official and other details, and throwing variety into his narrative by spirited sketches of the officers who distinguished themselves on both sides.—*Phila. Press.*

We have examined, with considerable care, the various works recently published, purporting to be accurate histories of the present civil war. We have compared them with each other upon such points as are most important, and we do most cheerfully accord to the work now before us, superiority in many essential respects.—*National Merchant.*

It is a thrilling history to read, and when these days of blood and war are passed, will be studied with the same mixture of wonder and of terror that we now feel in reading the story of our Revolutionary struggle, or any of the great tragedies of human history.—*Evangelist, New York.*

The work is not got up as a temporary and ephemeral production, by an unknown and irresponsible author, but is the result of careful and elaborate study, by an experienced writer, of established reputation, and acknowledged ability.—*Lutherian Observer, (Balt.)*

We would call the attention of our readers to the History of the Southern Rebellion, by Samuel M. Schmucker, L.L. D., which seems to be well worthy of public patronage. It is a beautiful volume, and the author is well known as a historian of no ordinary merit.—*Racine (Wis.) Advocate.*

We have thoroughly examined the work, and commend it to the careful perusal of all. Sparkling with rich, rare and racy incidents, full of valuable information, containing the fullest particulars, even to the most minute details of the rebellion up to the present time, replete with interest, censuring where censure is deserved, and applauding where merit is due, it is destined to become the most popular book of the times. Subscribe for the work, and our word for it you will not "buy a pig in a poke."—*Lancaster (O.) Gazette.*

We have before a copy of the History of the Rebellion, by S. M. Schmucker, LL.D., of Philadelphia. This we consider the most authentic, well and impartially written history of the war, which we have yet seen. The mechanical execution of the work, the paper, binding and illustrations are excellent, the steel engravings being executed by that eminent engraver, Samuel Sartain, Esq., and the subject matter all that the author claims, presenting a clear, concise and truthful account of the causes which led to the rebellion, all the civil and military events of importance that have occurred down to the end of the Peninsula campaign, together with biographical sketches of the various Commanders and Generals, both naval and military, who were the most prominent actors in the scenes up to that time. We cheerfully recommend the volume to all our readers, believing they will receive a full equivalent for their money.—*Watertown (Wis.) Democrat.*

www.ingramcontent.com/pod-product-compliance
Lightning Source LLC
Chambersburg PA
CBHW030317240426
43673CB00040B/1195